PERSONAL FINANCE
IN A PUBLIC WORLD

Janine and family,

Thanks for supporting your cousin's book

- Bobby

PERSONAL FINANCE IN A PUBLIC WORLD

HOW TECHNOLOGY, SOCIAL MEDIA, AND ADS AFFECT YOUR MONEY DECISIONS

BOB DEPASQUALE

NEW DEGREE PRESS

PERSONAL FINANCE IN A PUBLIC WORLD
How Technology, Social Media, and Ads Affect Your Money Decisions

ISBN   978-1-63730-665-9 *Paperback*
        978-1-63730-754-0 *Kindle Ebook*
        978-1-63730-868-4 *Ebook*

I dedicate this book to my family. Thank you for praying that my work might result in better lives for others.

Contents

Money and technology are tools for success.

Introduction

——

TIME AND MONEY

What would you prefer to have more of: time or money?

But time is money, right?

Let's run with that premise for a bit. Time is certainly valuable. Many say time is our most precious commodity. If that's the case, it's no wonder there is a never-ending technology race. Every tech company is trying to create something that saves us time. Speeding up tasks should, in theory, make the most desired experiences more enjoyable or, at a minimum, give us more time to enjoy them. That extra time should equal extra money. However, despite the speed technology gives us, we find ourselves busier than ever. We are moving faster but have more things to do and less time to do them. We look for more rather than looking to improve what we have. The desire to get ahead causes financial and emotional stress.

THE SPEED OF INFORMATION

I had my first experience with the speed of information transfer when my family got its first personal computer. Acquiring the device marked a momentous occasion. The only child my parents had was going to a private high school and would need a piece of modern technology to help with his education.

I wasn't overly interested in technology at that point in life, but we had some family friends who were in the business. They advised us on what type of computer to get and even set it up for us. We had a spare bedroom (benefits of having only one child) that was turned into an office, and shortly after converting the room we bought the new computer. Upon bringing it home, we had our friends come over. In less than an hour, they had everything up and running and even connected it to the internet! I was blown away. The thought of accessing information at the click of a button was fascinating. I was a curious kid, but not always motivated to research things in our hard copy *Encyclopedia Britannica*. The personal computer was going to revolutionize my thirteen-year-old life.

A dial-up modem and a phone line were needed to connect to the internet at the time. Our new computer came with a 28.8kbs (kilobits per second) modem. According to the Federal Communications Commission (FCC), today's low-end internet connection speeds are between three and eight megabits per second. One kilobit is 1/1,000th of a megabit. This means a "slow" internet connection from today is still 104 times faster than my 1990s life-changing machine. Technology has advanced at a rapid pace.

These days, we are all used to a different quality of information transfer. According to a 2019 report from Micro Focus, there are thirty-eight thousand status updates on Facebook every minute! Google processes over forty thousand search queries every second on average, which translates to over 3.5 billion searches per day and 1.2 trillion searches per year worldwide.

Priorities are extremely important when time is at a premium. Our minds tend to gravitate toward the things that stand out and are the most stimulating. We like to scroll through our Instagram feeds to see how our friends are doing. We check Snapchat to see their location. We learn how to dance and cook on TikTok. We get news from our favorite Facebook group and Tweet customer complaints. It's all too easy and time-consuming, but they're free! Or it seems like it, but they're actually costing us severely. Most of us don't pay for those services directly (LinkedIn is an example of a social networking site that does have a premium version), but we do pay for stuff. We buy what the advertisers on those applications are intentionally selling, and we buy what our digital connections are passively endorsing. There is a reason why Facebook had nearly $86 billion in revenue in 2020.

Companies are willing to pay a lot of money to catch our eyes and ears on social platforms. Those platforms have gathered billions of eyes and ears because we feed them our lives in an endless supply of content. Our public lives are making our personal financial situations suffer. We consume what's interesting freely and the foundational premises of good budgeting, risk management, investing, borrowing, lending, and economics don't catch our attention until it's too late. We are victims of overstimulation and greed. Chapter 1 examines how modern forms of media are more effective than the more traditional forms (such as television or radio) for advertisers.

Thankfully, there's a solution to our problem within immediate reach. In fact, it's what distracts us that will help us. We just need to prioritize our time. Then, if time is money, we'll be better off financially. Technology is the villain *and* the savior because it will not regress. The digital age is every age from here forward. With that being said, technology is not just for the newest things. It should also serve to make the traditional parts of life better. We should use it to make our financial lives stable before a benchmark to which we should compare our worth. If we can, our relationship with money will be healthy and our lives more joyful.

CREATIVE FINANCING

It was a big effort for me to gain acceptance into the prestigious St. Thomas Aquinas High School. While I probably didn't realize the importance at the time, I had to go through an interview process to be considered worthy of a private school education.

I was a typical teenager going through the motions during the process. I thought more about sports and my friends than the future of my life and the quality of my education. Looking back, it was a big commitment, and risk, for my parents. I went to the local middle school and rode my bike to get there. If accepted, I would have a forty-five-minute daily commute and a whole different level of responsibility. In addition, there was a cost to attend and my parents did not have enough money to pay the tuition, but we were resourceful. We had determination.

Ultimately, I was accepted, and we had just a few short weeks to prepare for the new school and year. My parents were determined to make it work financially and to support me in any way possible as I started a new chapter in life. To pay a reduced tuition rate, my mom took out a loan on her own account and paid the full tuition for my freshman year. I didn't know what she did at the time, but looking back, she did her research and the needed math to figure out it would be less expensive to get the yearly discount and pay back the loan. She thanks her years of working at a bank for enabling her to figure that out.

If my mom hadn't worked at a lending institution for much of the 1990s, I may not have received my education. She would have been unable to look up bank rates on the computer and compare different options. Today, she would just do an internet search.

We threw away our *Encyclopedia Britannica* a long time ago because we can find anything we want using our computer. You would think we would all be able to make wise decisions in every scenario. Unfortunately, decisions (especially those that are financially related) are made with emotions and their quality cannot be measured in megabits. It often takes major issues for us to change our habits, especially financial habits. Even then, the improved habits don't last forever.

In 2019, Northwestern Mutual published its tenth annual planning and progress study. The study explores US adults' attitudes and behaviors toward money, financial decision-making, and the broader issues impacting people's long-term financial security. The data was encouraging from a savings, debt, and retirement perspective.

- 71 percent feel financially secure today vs. only 47 percent who felt financially secure in 2009
- Compared to ten years ago:
    - 73 percent say their financial situation is better now
    - 88 percent say their financial habits are better
    - 74 percent are carrying less debt
    - 74 percent are more frugal
    - 66 percent have set specific goals for the next five to ten years, while only 57 percent said the same in 2009

This is certainly a positive result from the decade directly after the Great Recession, which started at the very end of 2007 and lasted until June of 2009. This was an extremely challenging eighteen-month period that had lasting effects even beyond 2009. Global gross domestic product decline was 5.1 percent and yielded 10 percent unemployment. Most people were affected drastically, and financial stress levels exploded. Media coverage was critical, and emotions were high. The time will never be forgotten, and people are still guided by their emotions from over a decade ago. Unfortunately, additional evidence suggests the foundational financial principles fall from our conscious the further we get from the major issue.

US consumer credit card debt was at an all-time high at over $930 trillion at the end of 2019, just before the COVID-19 pandemic hit. Despite the job losses, slower production, and other financial stressors, debt in early 2021 reduced to $773 trillion, suggesting again that more conservative money practices are initiated by extreme scenarios and desperation. This is not to say we can be fully prepared for or completely avoid events like the Great Recession and the coronavirus pandemic. We also cannot rely on government stimulus packages (which had a part in people paying down existing debt). These numbers do indicate the most stressful times bring out the most necessary behaviors. We have all of the data we could need, and we have lightning-fast ways to transfer it, but it takes the most extreme scenarios to yield the most responsible decisions.

We can use modern technology to help us make the healthiest financial decisions prior to the most devastating times. Preparation and prevention are key. I knew a few different people whose livelihood was greatly affected by COVID-19. The people I know who had budgeted well and had money to use in case of emergency were able to work through job losses or income drops well. Some people, including myself, founded businesses and used the extra time to start something new. In fact, this book likely would not exist if it wasn't for an effective emergency fund and free time.

We can set limits on our digital spending rather than rely on our willpower. We can research the quality of the things we purchase rather than try them out. We can also read thousands of reviews of a product or service we are considering instead of listening to the advertisement's excessive praise or trusting a stranger's well-positioned photo.

THE JOY OF TECHNOLOGY

I did not understand how my family's new computer worked when I started high school, but I enjoyed my newfound productivity. In fact, I enjoyed it so much that it became a toy. I had a sudden technology interest and a huge time suck. I spent the next four years using the computer sparingly for homework and primarily for playing games, researching sports, and looking for things I wanted. It's a good thing Amazon hadn't exploded yet or the family finances may have been strained more than they already were.

I became so interested in the computer that I noticed a 56k modem had been invented (Dr. Brent Townshend, 1996). I wanted more speed. I had no idea what "high-speed" internet would be like in college. During this rapid expansion of the internet, it was mostly looked at as a great new tool, but somewhere along the line, it took a major place in our lives. It's more than a tool now. It will be a net positive so long as we remain in control. We are all exposed to way more stimuli now than when I was as a teenager clogging up the phone line in the office.

The bombardment of information trains the brain to either ignore things or process them quickly to take in more information. In my experience with stimuli, unless under pressure (and eliciting a response from the amygdala), the mind tends to drift toward things that are enjoyable. Why would you want to experience something you don't enjoy if you don't have to? We're human. It's natural to choose joy. Unfortunately, it can take a Great Recession or viral pandemic to get us to address those not-so-enjoyable, yet valuable, things. In the absence of extreme urgency, and when your mind is overstimulated, it's easy to pass on the things you don't like. We can't let great financial practices fall into that category.

For example, if you're watching your favorite television show, you have a few options when it's commercial time. If you've recorded the show, you're in luck! Just fast forward through the advertisements (are you sensing a speed theme here?). If you are watching live, you'll have to either view the commercials or do something else to distract yourself until the show comes back on. You're more concerned about finishing the program efficiently so you can move on to another task, or maybe you're binge-watching an entire season. In which case, you'd have twenty episodes to squeeze in.

Here's how this scenario might impact your financial life. Let's says it's tax season and you know you're going to owe some money this year. You may not want to think about taxes during your favorite show. If an H&R Block commercial comes on, you're likely to do something else to avoid the discomfort of thinking about your tax situation. This is a reasonable action, but if the commercial led to you scheduling an appointment and avoiding future stress, it would be worthwhile. What if you opened a letter while you were watching the show that said you owed $10,000 in back taxes? Your first reaction might be that it's a fraud attempt. After that, you'd be likely to schedule your appointment with the tax representative.

STABILITY OVER VELOCITY

The year 2020 led me to many conversations about financial and emotional health. I realized there is no substitute for stability, and stability requires consistency. Those who have separated what they need from what they want appear to have the most consistent decision-making processes. They also have clearly defined what they want. It's not just "more" and "faster," which is an addictive style response. Their behaviors come from a place of satisfaction. They consume, but not in excess of their defined want. Their joy is not dictated by society or what any media source portrays. Perhaps the most powerful trait they have is the ability to "shop" without buying on impulse—a form of emotional control.

I believe with the ease of finding pleasurable stimuli, we are constantly distracting ourselves from valuable, sometimes more realistic, information and blurring the lines of needs and wants. A King Online University study says we tap, swipe, and click on our phone 2,617 times per day. Counterintuitively, technology is often "slowing" our progress and changing our decision-making processes. If time is money and our progress is slowed by technology, then technology is certainly changing the way we think about currency. I have determined if money and technology are very important parts of our lives, we must learn how to use them cohesively. If we do, our lives will be happier and healthier.

In this book, I will explain ways to efficiently manage your finances. You will learn important concepts that will help develop strong practices to guide your decision-making. Technology will still be a source of entertainment and productivity, but it will also help you manage your financial house well. It will feel great to scroll your social feeds contently. You will not feel a desire to replicate what your connections show. You'll know what you and your family need, and that will be enough. Making major purchasing decisions will be much easier and less time-consuming. You'll also have peace of mind in case of financial emergencies. Neither technology nor money will cause stress in your life because you will be in control.

1.

Thinking Is Habitual

PRIORITIZING YOUR UNIQUE SITUATION

When I was younger, one of my favorite activities was watching television on the couch with my father. It was typically sports and, if it was baseball season, it was almost definitely the New York Yankees. My dad was born and raised in New York, and I was also born there. It was kind of expected that I was a fan of New York sports teams—and specific ones, too.

My early childhood was not a very successful time for the Yankees. I would watch the games with my dad, but it was tough to get interested in a losing team. However, when the mid-nineties came, things would change. In 1996, the Yankees won their first World Series in eighteen years. This team was easy to enjoy. They had an incredible mix of young talent and great veteran ballplayers. One of those veterans was Wade Boggs.

When you're a kid, you tend to ask a lot of questions to your parents. By the end of the '96 season, Boggs was thirty-eight years old. He wasn't quite as good as he used to be, but he was still an All-Star that year. He was the type of player my dad really admired—not flashy, but consistent. One evening, I remember asking my dad why he was so good, and he didn't have a great answer other than, "He does the 'little things.'" Right on cue, the announcer in the game we were watching mentioned some of Boggs's habits.

Boggs was known for fielding exactly 150 groundballs prior to games, starting his batting practice at exactly 5:17 p.m. (during night games) and running wind sprints at exactly 7:17 p.m. That's meticulous, but perhaps even more extreme was he would eat chicken before every game. Since 1961, every team in the league has played 162 games per season. For Boggs, that's an incredible amount of chicken over an eighteen-year major league career. He felt most comfortable doing his job when executing these habits. In some strange way, such detailed preplanning provided the comfort he needed to play an extremely reactionary sport.

When I was younger, I would gather information from television. I grew up in the "SportsCenter Age" where that was the best place to get your sports news. You are likely to have seen a SportsCenter commercial if you have ever watched ESPN. I am sure I was influenced by whatever messages ESPN and their advertisers wanted to present. I habitually watched the channel and was exposed to whatever was aired. I wonder if I spent as much time watching ESPN as Wade Boggs did fielding ground balls or eating pregame chicken.

Habits are an amazing thing. They can become so natural we do not even realize they exist. It's as if the more we do them, the less noticeable they are. Ideally, we would all develop great habits related to our money decisions. We would get to the point where the habits are so ingrained that they are unnoticeable.

I am sure the more Wade completed his program ritual, the harder it would have been to avoid it. The same could be said for me and my television watching habits. We all have habits that were established at a young age.

FORMING HABITS

Young people have developing minds. An adult brain acts differently than an adolescent's brain. It is said the average person's brain is not fully developed until age twenty-five. A brain's way of acting is thinking. Therefore, it's not always easy to identify a brain's habits. It might be fully developed before its habits are even noticed. However, prior to full development, it is much more impressionable, and there are opportunities to train it.

The small patterns we develop when we are young stick with us for life. It's hard to kick any twenty-five-year habit, no less one that formed our brain's foundation. In his book *Atomic Habits*, James Clear calls this the "habit loop." It consists of a cue, a craving, a response, and a reward. He says, "This four-step process is not something that happens occasionally, but rather is an endless feedback loop that is running and active during every moment that you are alive." It happens in an instance, which is partially why it's hard to break the pattern.

The ways children gather information today are much different than the previous generations. Modern technology allows information to be acquired at the push of a button. Opinions can be shared in the same manner. Studying is "searching" and writing is typing. Entertainment is on-demand. Games are web-based. There's even E-sports (although, I wouldn't call that physical exercise). Habits have changed drastically.

When I was growing up, and not watching the Yankees with my dad, I would make phone calls to my friends in the neighborhood to see if they were available to come over to my house and hang out. Nowadays, we have electronically scheduled playdates through an online calendaring system.

We'll move on to avoid a nostalgic memoir, but it must be noted that each generation has a different developmental experience that molds their minds.

The most recent shift in learning revolves around curiosity and satisfaction. One thing that hasn't changed in my life is that I like communicating and hanging out with my friends. I'm sure I'll always enjoy those activities. The difference is it is now much easier to reach that satisfaction. I don't have to call my friend on a landline (What did they do before phones?) to see if he's around. I could either text him or check Instagram for a story update. My brain is trained to "click" and move on. It's predisposed to expect immediate results. This is unique to people my age and younger. We've spent most of our lives in that environment and don't know any different.

Interestingly, the habits I formed when I was younger have made my childhood phone numbers stick with me. We moved when I was in seventh grade, and so I have two phone numbers and two addresses I had to memorize and recite consistently. They'll stick with me forever. What's your child-hood number? I bet you can think of it right away.

TECHNOLOGY THE TOOL

Curiosity often leads to discovery, but it can also lead to frustration and otherwise detrimental actions. Managing expectations is important, but beyond allowing for more time to find answers, what else can we do to have more positive information-gathering experiences?

My encouragement is that you already have valuable information. Technology should be used as a tool and not a guide. Its role is manifested through the psychological habits you form.

For example, your best friend's recent social media post from their international vacation is a great *tool* for you to see what and how they are doing. It is not a *guide* as to what you should be doing or where you should be.

Psychologically, it's a much different experience to be happy for your friend than to be jealous of them. I must acknowledge there is a spectrum, but where you land on it greatly affects your well-being.

It's critical to exercise habits that elicit feelings of fulfillment and appreciation, not desire and frustration. If you need a shift in mindset, it may take some time. In *Atomic Habits*, Clear also stresses the importance of small improvements to your habits. You cannot expect massive change to come rapidly. He says, "It can take years before it happens all at once," meaning you will eventually recognize the results of consistent small actions. Clear calls it the "plateau of latent potential." If you can reach that plateau, your efforts suddenly become more rewarding and recognizable. People start acknowledging your progress, and you begin to feel better about what you've done.

I find that learning a musical instrument illustrates the plateau of latent potential well. The early stages of practicing, especially for the average person, can be extremely frustrating. You must practice skills and techniques first. Guitar players have to practice finger agility, pianists practice finger dexterity, saxophonists work on breathing, and percussionists exercise limb independence. Without the basics, you cannot create music, and the basics take time. Muscles and joints tire easily. Therefore, you cannot power through a training session. In fact, overtraining and injury are possible. Gradual improvements must be made to reach the plateau. Eventually, your latent potential seems to arise, and you realize the consistent hard work has paid off.

THE INTERNAL PROCESSES

We've been analyzing external communication. We must also consider internal communication and what's actually happening when you feel better about something. Dopamine is one of the main methods of communication inside your body. It relates to many bodily functions, including your heart rate, sleeping, motivation, blood flow, and attention. It's what is called a neurotransmitter, or a messenger inside the brain. In some cases, it can be used as a life-saving medical treatment. Modern technology isn't all that bad! You may have heard of people searching for "dopamine hits" in the digital world.

This is because it is often associated with pleasurable actions. While it's not solely related to things generally considered enjoyable, it's natural to seek its byproducts. It feels good when someone "likes" your post. So, what do you do? You post more things people will like. You solicit approval, and the more you get, the more you need. At a certain point, you begin experiencing immunity, and you either do more or move on to something else.

You're probably thinking, "What's wrong with seeking harmless pleasure?" Nothing. Don't worry. This is not a referendum on enjoyment. In fact, I encourage it. I just prefer it be rooted in your own thoughts and not assumed expectations.

It has been proven that dopamine is released prior to an enjoyable experience. In other words, you actually experience your greatest pleasure when thinking about an impending experience. Isn't it exciting to think about a great vacation? How pumped-up were you before your last speaking engagement or sports competition? It's the idea of success that often pushes you through challenging times and yields tremendous effort.

SEEKING A PLEASURABLE EXPERIENCE

There are a lot of indications that we continue to seek pleasure at a faster pace. Many people and companies are capitalizing on this premise by consistently presenting the most dopamine-worthy content. The consistent nature keeps us coming back.

The advent of the social media tech company has added a third party to the advertising equation. Marketing and sales have changed. Zig Ziglar once said, "You can have everything in life you want if you will just help enough other people get what they want." This offers great motivation for a salesperson to provide what a client needs. It's a simple relationship. There are two main parties: the consumer and the company.

These days, the salesperson has been replaced by the social media tech company. The product company still sells its products, but it accesses the customer through the tech company, which is not an employee dedicated to sales. As much as the two companies work together, they operate differently. The salesperson delivers a product; the tech company delivers an experience.

We value experiences more than things. My nieces and nephew have a bunch of replaceable Disney toys, but a select few trips to Disneyland that they'll never forget.

Consider *The Experience Economy* by B. Joseph Pine II and James H. Gilmore. The authors posit that the best companies stage incredible experiences for their customers. It is no longer sufficient to simply provide a good product or excellent service. Customers may appreciate what was given to or done for them, but they are not likely to come back simply for those reasons.

For example, my earliest memories of the dentist are very positive, whereas I often hear of the fears people have when going to the dentist. It's partially because I had healthy teeth, but the primary reason I liked the dentist was because of the "kid's" section in the waiting room. It was full of puzzles, games, and other entertaining things.

Most people go to the dentist to get their teeth cleaned or because something is wrong. The dentist they go to might be excellent at their job, but they only go there if the service is needed. Young Bobby, on the other hand, used to ask his mother when they would have the opportunity to go back. I wanted to go back to the "kid's" area because the experience was enjoyable.

THE ATTENTION BUSINESS

In one way, the existence of three parties is beneficial to us consumers. We get two companies trying to provide us with things we want, but two is not always better than one. In this case, it's important to identify the difference between wants and needs. We'll dive deeper into this in Chapter 5. For now, it's safe to assume much of our social media consumption is unnecessary entertainment. It's an enjoyable experience, and enjoyment is good for our mental health, but it's not essential. This is different from having a nice experience at the dentist, which should be considered a necessary service. Experiences could also be distracting us from something more important, in which case it's not only exposing us to the enticing advertisements, but also preventing us from doing something to advance our own well-being (like brushing our teeth).

The third party in the above equation exists for the purpose of gathering our attention. It's a business and needs to generate revenue and appease shareholders. It does this by proving to advertisers that its platform is frequently and consistently used by as many people as possible. It will create whatever experience will maximize your engagement. The algorithms behind today's social technology are incredibly intelligent and they prove to advertisers that their messages will be seen on the platform. Advertisers are willing to pay massive amounts of money to be seen.

It is important to understand how the brain works before applying specific concepts. You will be more equipped to make your own decisions with a base understanding of the brain's processes and how you experience today's technology.

Throughout the text, we will cover various aspects of personal finance and apply the rules of the modern world. You will learn how to develop healthy financial habits and use technology as a tool to assist in the process. As a result, you will be able to enjoy the experiences that are provided at the touch of a button or swipe of a screen while being confident your immediate enjoyment will not lead to adverse long-term effects.

The goal is for you to prioritize your own situation before using the tools (not guides) that technology has provided us to make wise decisions for yourself and your family.

2.

Chasing the Money

UNDERSTANDING SOCIAL TECHNOLOGY AND RETARGETING ADS

We all have that friend in life who we can reconnect with as if no time passed between meetings. You talk about things like they happened just yesterday. You may even reminisce about some life-changing events you experienced together.

I have learned it is also good to ask old friends about how things are going at the moment. People like to know you care about how they are doing. It's amazing how quickly you can catch up on things, though. It's also amazing how little time it takes for their interests to impact your social media experience and influence your buying habits these days.

THE NEW OVEN I DIDN'T NEED

I remember a specific conversation I had with an old friend from college. It was about twenty years after we went to school together. Most of our conversation was about what life used to be like and how we made it to the present. One of the things we joked about was the quality of the food in the college cafeteria. Let's just say it provided some calories and probably not too many vitamins and minerals.

Speaking of vitamins and minerals, we were both healthy adults at the time of our conversation, and by then there were some pretty slick appliances to help you cook great meals in short periods of time. I happen to enjoy cooking, so an old-fashioned stove top and oven serve me well. My friend lives a more fast-paced lifestyle, and small, quick, healthy meals are important. He had just moved to a different state and was in a new apartment for only a week and expected to move again shortly. Needless to say, fast food would have been the simple choice for most.

While we were catching up, my friend told me he was cooking dinner. I figured he wasn't tearing up the kitchen with an apron and a chef's hat, but he did say he was making chicken and vegetables. When I asked, he said he was using a mini-oven to cook. Being an inspired chef, I pried a bit. It was a Brava oven. Naturally, I went right to the internet to look it up. I spent about two minutes on the website. It looked like a pretty interesting item, but that was it. We went back to our conversation and eventually wrapped up (after he burnt the chicken).

I fell asleep shortly after our conversation. When I woke up the next morning, something interesting happened. I felt like I was being watched, or targeted. I checked my phone to see what I missed in the past eight hours (like a typical millennial). The first thing I saw was a Brava advertisement!

The third thing I saw was Brava. I switched applications, and guess what popped up? Yes, the new mini-oven I had to have.

I had long since hypothesized that we are more likely to make buying decisions based on what we see on the internet. However, I hadn't thought about how much we dictate what we see. I am in a much better financial position in my life now than when my friend and I were college students, but I denied myself the new oven with a determination to not fit into my hypothesis. It likely would not have ruined my budget for the month, but there was a much more productive use of $800.

I now have a whole new idea of how ad targeting works. The internet displays what we see, but *we* actually dictate the content.

HOW RETARGETING ADS WORK

Retargeting ads are used by companies to "follow" visitors to their websites around the internet. Most sources will state that users spend about fifteen seconds on a website. That's not saying much for our attention spans. Advertisers know this, so they try to gather information about users' browsing tendencies in a rather successful attempt to follow us around the internet. One way they do this is by the use of cookies. Who doesn't love cookies (the unhealthy, baked type)?

Internet cookies are small pieces of information that are stored by your web browser and provide information about your browsing history. You may see a lot of sites these days giving a warning or asking you to accept their use of cookies. Most of us will simply click "okay" to move on to the content. After all, you have to satisfy your brain in fifteen seconds, right?

Cookies can be helpful to make your browser load pages faster because it already has some information stored. It's always about speed—the faster, the better. Supposedly, it's better for the user and it is better for a sites' ranking on search engines. However, that information your browser saves also provides information about you.

Brava knew I had been to its site the night before. It was ready to "pounce" on me once I pulled up any social media application the next morning. I was not all that upset, just a little startled. I could see why someone would have purchased the appliance right there. It wasn't the right time while on the phone with a long-lost friend the night before, though it was something I would like. I certainly didn't chase it. In fact, it chased me.

What I failed to tell you originally was the friend who told me about the oven was a social media advertisement expert. His name is Joe Nolan, and he's the founder and CEO of JoNo Marketing. When I told him about my experience a few days later, he laughed. It was something he sees every day. He's represented some of the largest brands in the world, and their goal was to target their ideal customers who have already shown an interest in their product or service.

In future conversations with Joe, I asked him more about the process. He said the advertisers are able to reach the consumer with tremendous precision. They find the right people, use a relevant message, and deliver it at the right time. He mentioned Google's Zero Moment of Truth (ZMOT), or the moment in the buying process when the consumer researches a product prior to purchase.

Joe stressed, "Never before has there been that level of precision. From the strategy side all the way down to the execution." People used to see advertisements in the newspaper, on television, or hear them on the radio. Companies would talk about their sales and try to drive attention to their product or service. Networks would choose what we see based mostly on the amount of money an advertiser was willing to pay (there was some filter provided by morality and the Federal Communications Commission). It was easy to tune them out or turn the page away from something you weren't interested in. Now, it's an enjoyable user experience. We like being marketed to!

DIGITAL ADDICTION

Times are different now. We spend enormous amounts on electronic devices (they are a major personal financial decision on their own), and ads are designed just for those devices. We are being told to buy all day long as applications feed us what we are interested in, but why do we accept this? Who wants to see advertisements all day long? We are okay with it because we *have* to display much of our lives on social media platforms and we desire feedback.

In *Irresistible*, Adam Alter says, "Hundreds of millions of people share their lives in real-time through Instagram posts, and just as quickly those lives are evaluated in the form of comments and likes." Those responses often illicit dopamine. We love being "online."

Alter also references the thoughts of a key employee at one of the most popular applications. "Greg Hochmuth, one of Instagram's founding engineers, realized he was building an engine for addiction. 'There's always another hashtag to click on,' Hochmuth said. 'Then it takes on its own life like an organism and people can become excessive. Instagram, like so many other social media platforms, it's bottomless.'"

Alter continues by quoting Tristan Harris from the Center for Humane Technology. "The problem isn't that people lack willpower. It's that there are 1000 people on the other side of the screen whose job it is to break down the self-regulation you have." In other words, there are technology professionals who are employed to take advantage of our human addictive tendencies. App users can be addicts in their own right, and according to Alter, "addiction is produced largely by environment and circumstance." Consequently, there is a professionally developed custom environment designed to feed our behavioral addictions.

Our personal financial situations are not taken into consideration by the engineers that develop applications. Their goal is to keep us on the platforms which feed us tempting advertisements.

Ironically, even some wise, money-saving financial decisions can feed us additional ads. How many applications of which do you use the free version? Ever listen to music on YouTube? Your "fee" for these actions is watching (or listening to) commercials. If you want the ad-free version, you'll have to pay $5 a month (this would be a way to eliminate one of the three parties, but still at a cost).

YOUR OWN PERSONAL ADVERTISEMENT PLAYLIST

Many of the ads (like the Brava oven) we see are for things we have already identified as interesting. Our environments and circumstances are following us, and advertisers are one step more efficient. They can target people who show a predisposition to purchasing their product or service. In one way, this is great for all parties because it wastes less time. Honestly, I'd rather see a Brava commercial than one for fast food. At the same time, it also means I could easily rack up quite a credit card bill if I bought everything I see that interests me.

It is as if we are always shopping in a superstore like Target or Walmart. A variety of all the things we like is rotating through our social feeds, and it takes but a few taps or clicks to execute a purchase. This is in contrast to previous forms of advertising (i.e., newspaper, magazine, or billboard) that were not specifically targeted to the viewer and did not allow for the immediate satisfaction of a "buy now" button. You can't swipe your credit card in a magazine.

In my conversation with my friend Joe, he referenced some of the tools different digital platforms have. Twitter acquired MoPub in 2013. Google has its Display Network and Facebook has its Audience Network. These huge platforms have developed or bought software systems designed to make audience targeting as easy as possible. In Joe's previous roles and at his current company, he and his colleagues are tasked with managing these software across platforms.

Perhaps the most powerful concept in the whole system is that every consumer will experience a finite number of ad impressions. There is only so much time in the day and so much content one can consume. This limited supply has made the commodity the platforms have extremely valuable. Advertisers are willing to pay an increasing amount for it. Joe also pointed out advertisers are competing across industries because of the sophistication of the software. A small kitchen appliance is not the only thing I am likely (according to my internet habits) to buy. I am sure Home Depot or Nike would gladly replace Brava's oven ads.

I encourage you to experiment with letting a family member or someone you live with use your device for browsing one night (or even a few). See what type of advertisements you see during that period. First of all, you'll notice a difference. Secondly, you'll probably learn a little bit about the person you let use your device.

COMBATING THE ADDICTING FORCES

Today's technology cannot, nor should it, be avoided. You should use it for good. There are many fine personal financial tools and concepts that must be prioritized. To do that, you'll have to combat the addicting forces.

We have identified two major forces at work: digital behavioral addiction and advertisement retargeting. The first is a product of our human nature. Alter provides numerous examples of experiments designed to examine addictive behavior. The key premise is behavioral addictions are strikingly similar to substance addictions. He claims, "Time has made a fool of the experts who once believed that addiction was reserved for a wretched minority." In contrast, addictive behaviors are actually expressed by the majority. While events may not rise to the extreme level of substance abuse, it is the consistent application that drives effectiveness. This is why social applications are successful.

Alter continues, "People were addicted to substances, not behaviors. The feedback they got from behaviors alone couldn't ever rise to the euphoric intensity of injected heroin, but just as drugs have become more powerful over time, so has the thrill of behavioral feedback. Product designers are smarter than ever. They know how to push our buttons and how to encourage us to use their products not just once, but over and over."

It is the "over and over" that leads to the second force. We will keep coming back. It's not a hard decision for an advertiser to show up where we'll be. Statista reported $325 billion was spent on digital advertising worldwide in 2019 (prior to the COVID-19 pandemic). About $614 billion was spent on advertising in total. Digital already accounts for more than half of the amount of money companies spend globally. With television seeming to have peaked and other major forms like newspapers, radio, and magazines experiencing significant declines, the digital ad age is clearly upon us.

Many projections put the digital total above two-thirds of the total spend within the next couple of years. Why pay for a billboard ad on a highway when we spend way more time scrolling our phone than driving? Hopefully, you don't do them simultaneously. It would, however, be nice if you could limit your digital screen time to be similar to that of the amount the average person spends driving. In 2019, The Car Connection noted the typical American spends about fifty-two minutes driving a day. I challenge you to a day of less than one hour of leisure screen time.

IF YOU CAN'T ABSTAIN, MAKE IT A HEALTHY HABIT

If we apply James Clear's principles from *Atomic Habits*, it's possible to train the brain to consistently make wise technology-related decisions that will compound over time. He provides four laws of behavior change to create a good habit: make it obvious, make it attractive, make it easy, and make it satisfying. These can be inverted to break a bad habit. Alter claims breaking the habit may not always be a possible option when related to digital media in today's world because "Abstinence isn't an option. But there are other alternatives." He suggests keeping social media applications in one "corner" of your life, as his research indicates addictive behaviors are a product of one's environment.

Once you've identified the appropriate time period for digital consumption, proceed with the inversion of the laws of behavior change. Make the habit invisible, unattractive, difficult, and unsatisfying. For example, if the site or sounds of your phone trigger you to scroll your Twitter account, hide it from yourself. Second, identify the reasons why you don't want to use the phone, such as wasting time or spending money. Then, make it difficult to actually do any of those things by setting restrictions on usage time, blocking certain websites, changing passwords, or deleting credit cards from applications. Finally, make it unsatisfying by creating drawbacks or mini punishments for using it at the wrong time.

One example practice would be to not allow yourself to charge your phone until you sleep. If you drain the battery during the day, you get less time to use it later in the day when it's not a distraction, or in its "corner." If you can close the bad habit loop and consistently limit your app usage to a certain time of day (or week), you will develop a healthy loop, systematically avoid the environment of temptation, and lower your overall exposure to ad impressions.

You'll find with lower ad exposure you'll be less tempted to purchase unneeded items. You'll also have fewer decisions to make and find yourself to be less disappointed for lack of possessions. Time is better spent in forms of edification and entertainment. Fewer advertisements mean more availability for the things that bring you joy. Also, when you concentrate less on what you could potentially have, you appreciate what you do have so much more, and you're more aware of what actually needs to be replaced. You might save yourself some money and have enough to fix or replace something that is truly a need. Therefore, you can improve your quality of life by eliminating some short-term distractions, avoiding advertisements, and saving your money for wiser purchases.

Great habits are the foundation for managing your personal finances in today's digital world. Work to make it as natural as possible for yourself.

CONTROLLING YOUR DEVICES

In addition to your own habits, there are some simple steps to tweaking the "habits" of your devices if retargeting and cookies make you feel uncomfortable or are too effective in leading you to make purchases. Most sites will allow you to disallow cookies or customize the settings. This will control individual sites.

Another good practice is to periodically wipe your browser's history or cache. This removes the cookies and eliminates the data your browser has stored about you. This is not the only thing you'll need to do because social media applications have their own settings. They often position the information they share with their "partners" as a way to make your browsing experience more enjoyable. You may feel that way, but if not, you can adjust the settings to your liking. Make the technology work as hard as you do to foster the best environment for sound financial decisions.

It is important to understand how much technology understands our thought processes as you work through this text. It will help you understand how to make wise decisions across all financial topics. The goal is to identify specific areas of finance, how the digital world relates to each area, and how we can use technology to assist in making wise personal financial decisions.

3.

A Quick Buck

———

HOW NOT TO GET RICH

I used to check on my friend's dogs when he and his family were out of town. One of the dogs would be so excited to eat that it could make itself throw up. You would think it would have eventually figured out a slower approach to eating was more effective. I contrast that with my cat who we give a few days' worth of food before a long weekend away. He seems to ration it perfectly.

Are you able to ration your income? Budgeting your finances is a long-term process. There are no overnight successes.

The foundational practice of growing your financial worth is saving. You must have more money coming in than flowing out. While this practice is not a complicated concept, it often slips past our conscious. We tend to come up with other ways we'd like to build financial wealth. While I don't believe financial wealth ultimately brings us fulfillment, it can bring short-term joy. In fact, I think it's often healthy to "treat" ourselves to certain luxuries. Unfortunately, that isn't often good enough. We tend to want more and try to find the best of both worlds. We want the immediate pleasure of the "treat" plus the benefits of a consistent savings and investment habit. There are a few ways to do this.

HOW TO GET A "GOOD DEAL"

The least advisable way to solve all of your financial desires would be some sort of fraudulent or extremely risky scheme. The problems here are obvious, and most don't choose this route. The other two options, however, are prevalent.

One way to chase a financial windfall is gambling or playing the lottery. Casino.org reported almost $72 billion was spent in the US alone on lottery tickets in 2017. Powerball total ticket sales per draw are consistently above ten million, often closer to twenty, and can reach above one hundred million if the pot is extremely high. It seems like a worthwhile $2 expenditure, but the chances of winning the lottery are slim. Florida Lottery's website says, for its Mega Millions game, the overall odds of winning a prize are 1 in 24, and the odds of winning the jackpot are 1 in 302,575,350. Compared to those odds, Investopedia offers these probabilities where you have a:

- one in 2,320,000 chance of being killed by lightning.
- one in 3,441,325 chance of dying after coming into contact with a venomous animal or plant.
- one in ten million chance of being struck by falling airplane parts.

You have a greater chance of suffering these tragedies than of winning the lottery. It's not a great way to plan your financial present or future.

What if you're a smart shopper? The third way you might find an immediate financial advantage is presented to us more than we seek it. There will always be times in which we celebrate the expensive things we have, but it has also become popular to celebrate the sale. Everyone loves a buy-one-get-one (BOGO). You can't make it through the supermarket these days without something being on sale. The red stickers jump out at you. There are "discount" auto sellers, discount convenience stores; there are even discount brokerages for investors. The problem is just because something is a good "deal" or on sale doesn't mean it's a good use of your money, especially for long-term financial wealth building. You're still spending money, and unless it's not something you truly need, in the long run it may not be worth the effect on your bottom line.

Even the greatest of luxuries are participating in the discount economy. Commercial aviation is a great example of the modern world. It's easier than ever to hop on a flight to most places around the globe. Discount airlines have made travel more consistent for a lot of people. You could make travel a line item in your budget and not sacrifice all of your discretionary dollars. It could also be easy to "nickel and dime" yourself into debt with weekend getaways. Southwest Airlines asks a rhetorical question in their marketing efforts: "Wanna get away?" Yes! Of course, we want to get away...and save money at the same time. It's so easy. Just buy a ticket.

THE SLIDING $1

One of my most memorable travel experiences illustrates our desire to acquire money in the easiest way possible. I attended college in Long Island, New York, and grew up outside of Fort Lauderdale, Florida. Thanks to Southwest Airlines, I could get home a couple of times a year in just a few hours. It cost me about $200 for a round trip, and bags flew free (they still do in 2021). The lowest-cost itineraries often had a stop between ISP (Long Island McArthur Airport) and FLL (Ft. Lauderdale Hollywood International Airport).

At the end of my junior year, I was excited to head home for a couple of weeks. I had booked a Southwest flight out of ISP that landed at BWI (Baltimore Washington International Thurgood Marshall Airport) for a long layover before my connecting flight departed for FLL. I knew I was going to get in very late. The flight was cheap. The layover wasn't ideal. I planned on entertaining myself by walking around the airport and window shopping.

The first leg of the journey was pretty routine. We took off late in the morning and got to BWI around 1:00 p.m. Upon arriving, I gathered my carry-on (this was back when there was enough room in the overhead compartment) and headed out to the terminal. My typical routine was to find my gate immediately and make sure everything was copacetic. I knew this airport well and was confident I would be able to locate the gate for the next flight. I just needed to find the screen with the list of departures and gates.

When I exited the jetway, I was greeted by what seemed like a thousand people. I had never seen an airport so busy.

Every seat at the gate was taken, and there was a line at the desk. It was loud and somewhat disorienting. I navigated people hustling to and from their gates and made it across the main walkway over to the bathrooms. I thought I'd be able to gather myself there, but to my dismay, the bathroom was just as packed.

I survived the bathroom and slid along the wall that led to the monitors I needed to check. Thankfully, I wasn't rushed because I knew I had plenty of time before my next flight. I made it to a point under the monitors. I couldn't actually see what they read. I had to contort my body while using the weight of my luggage to balance and see the screen. Of course, my gate was number three. It was at the far end of the terminal.

I had given up my desire to walk around the terminal at this point and just wanted to sit down. I set out on a ten-minute walk to my gate. It felt like I was tiptoeing and making sure my bag didn't roll over anyone's feet. I found myself speeding up to the pace of everyone rushing around me and finally saw gate three in the distance. I felt the need to run up to the counter and beg to get on my flight as if it was leaving. However, I sighed and was content with being hours ahead of my scheduled departure.

My next task was to find a seat. Frustration built again. There was nowhere to sit at this end of the terminal, either. This was also before charging stations were popular. Prime charging real estate was overcrowded. I ended up finding a spot against a wall that I could sit and lean against.

Sitting on the floor is terribly uncomfortable for me. This one was hard tile and was clearly well-traveled. I had my eye on the seating area. Eventually, a group stood up, and I jumped up and darted over to their seats. I was able to acquire their prime spot facing the main walkway. I love people-watching, and this was a fair consolation prize to window shopping throughout the terminal.

Once I sat down and got settled, it seemed like things suddenly slowed down. It was my luck that now I could more easily walk around. I wasn't about to give up the spot I had scouted and for which I sat on the hard floor. I was prepared to get comfortable and maybe even take a nap.

Shortly thereafter, I noticed someone was stumbling in the middle of the walkway. I almost got up expecting them to fall over, but they kept their balance and kept on moving. There was a group of teenagers sitting on the floor against the wall opposite to where I was originally sitting. They were overly amused by the person stumbling. I realized they had something to do with it. There were four of them. Once there was a lull in the foot traffic, two of them got up, circled around, and walked down the walkway. The kid on the left dropped something (on purpose) and they peeled off and covertly, or not so covertly, went back and sat down by their friends. One of the kids that didn't get up was holding the end of a string that was connected to what was dropped in the middle of the walkway.

These teenagers created the ultimate airport terminal prank. For the next hour, they provided entertainment for anyone who was waiting for a flight. There were 5 gates within range to see what was going on. Hundreds of people watched as an unexpecting "lucky" person would be rushing through the terminal and find a dollar bill just sitting on the ground. The poor traveler would inevitably slow down (not stop), bend over, and try to pick up a bill that would slide along the floor. They'd keep after it for a few steps and realize that it's not a gust of wind that's making the bill move. I sat there along with most of the other people waiting for flights and had the most entertaining layover I've ever experienced. There were multiple times the whole terminal filled with laughter as someone tried to pick up the money.

We all want to make a quick buck. It's easy. It provides instant gratification. While making a lot of money in a short period of time often entails illegal activity coming at the expense of someone else, the low probability of winning the lottery is just as unattractive. They are different, but neither is a sustainable model for financial management. It may seem that it's the way to get rich or live your dreams, but it just isn't the case. In fact, even if you do win the lottery, it's not likely you'll be rich forever. The *Washington Post* reported in 2019 that 70 percent of people who receive a large windfall or win the lottery end up going broke. This shows sudden wealth isn't always the answer.

THE MOST FAMOUS PONZI SCHEME

Perhaps the best proof that making large amounts of money, whether fraudulently or by luck, doesn't actually curb someone's desire for more is in the story of Bernie Madoff. Madoff coordinated the largest Ponzi scheme ever. He did all this after having what just about anyone would consider a successful financial career. He was making about $100 million per year.

In 1990, Madoff became the chairman of NASDAQ and also served in the role in 1991 and 1993. He had plenty of power and influence. He was known for being a very determined businessman and found his motivation by playing the "small firm" role. He was willing to complete transactions that were typically considered too small for the average investment firm at the time. Similar to Michael Jordan finding motivation from being cut from his high school basketball team, Bernie convinced himself he was the underdog.

It's not exactly clear when the fraudulent activity occurred, but Madoff has stated it started in 1991. In the scheme, Madoff's fund would promise returns to investors and collect millions of dollars in fees as if the funds were actually being invested. In reality, employees were told to generate fake trade statements and the money was made to seem legitimate. Madoff relied on his connections and reputation to continue to bring in new money. People wanted to be part of his fund. There was FOMO (fear of missing out) before the acronym even existed.

People were allowed to withdraw money from their accounts, but these transactions were funded by inflows from new investors. The scheme lasted until 2008 (which was seventeen years based on Madoff's stated beginning date of 1991), at which point the Great Recession caused things to collapse. The firm could not keep up with the amount of money from redemptions that were being requested.

Madoff told Steve Fishman, the author of *Ponzi Supernova*, via phone while he was incarcerated, "I had more than enough money to support any of my lifestyle and my family's lifestyle. I didn't need to do this for that." He had enough money. More would not have satisfied him.

Interestingly, Madoff had the long-term financial success many people dream of, but he still had the "quick buck" mentality. He created an unsustainable (and fraudulent) system that played to his desire to acquire more money more swiftly, and he couldn't avoid the habit loop.

WANTING MONEY, HAVING STUFF, AND NEEDING TIME

Morgan Housel in his book *The Psychology of Money* says, "When most people say they want to be a millionaire, what they might actually mean is, 'I'd like to spend a million dollars,' and that is literally the opposite of being a millionaire." The quick buck we want to make is actually not what we want. So, why try to acquire it if we're just going to spend it?

Madoff was way beyond a millionaire. How could he have wanted more money? He certainly didn't need it. His fortune was some sort of status symbol and measurement of self-worth over net worth.

The philosopher Ayn Rand once said, "Money is only a tool. It will take you wherever you wish, but it will not replace you as the driver." Money is only a means to an end. It is up to us to decide how we go about acquiring it and what we are working toward.

We have all been asked, "What would you buy if you won the lottery?" The answer is usually something extravagant like a mansion or an exotic car. As fun as the thought of winning the lotto is, I don't like the question. It gives a sense that a financial windfall is more likely than it really is, and that spending is what rich people do. It's similar to the coveting of what we see on our "feeds." It may not be to the scale of a $100 million lottery prize, but we spend hundreds and thousands of hours scrolling for what we would do with our winnings. The method of acquisition is unlikely, but the desire for the "stuff" is present. Immediate satisfaction does not belong in a healthy financial plan, no matter the amount of money involved. The best financiers know this.

Housel says of one of the most famous investors, Warren Buffett, "His skill is investing, but his secret is time."

We must take advantage of the time value of money, meaning the sooner you begin saving, the longer it will have time to grow. If you buy a $5 coffee today, it might taste great or have even given you a boost of energy. If you save that $5, it could be worth $6 (a 20 percent gain) next year, and $7.20 the following year. In ten years, it would be worth $25 at that pace. That is an aggressive pace, but even a 5 percent return yearly would yield you $7.75. Imagine if you saved that $5 every day. Limit immediate gratifications to build gratification that is not only deferred but also stronger. I'd rather have the money I have today plus some tomorrow than whatever short-term indulgence is on my mind.

The best way to manage one's finances and build wealth is over time. You have to be consistent (*Atomic Habits* apply).

You need stability and you need to follow basic principles. Housel quotes Voltaire when he says, "History never repeats itself, but man always does." Hopefully, we repeat wise money decisions despite ever-changing investments, rules, and money standards.

Housel also says, "How you behave is also more important than what you know." It's great to have a lot of knowledge, but consistent application of the basic principles is most important. Voltaire assures us times will change, but we can be stable. Housel states it's more important we act on what we know than trying to find the next best strategy. Saving more than you earn will always be a relevant strategy.

WHEN COMPACT DISCS WERE THE TEMPTING TECHNOLOGY

It used to be sufficient to refrain from dialing the phone number from an "As Seen on TV" advertisement or disposing of the "annual catalog." In most cases, that was easy enough. I spent much of my adolescence saving the little money I had (this is past the piggy bank stage described in Chapter 4). However, I have one confession.

When I was in high school, I succumbed to the pressure, or maybe it was my parents who succumbed to my pressure. I saw one too many Columbia House commercials. I think I paid one cent for twelve music albums on compact disc and was put in a club and forced to buy another twenty at some point. In actuality, we did the math and wouldn't have done it if it wasn't a reasonable deal, but I was definitely sold by the consistent exposure. Once again, it was consistency showing its power. I triumphed in the end, though.

Ironically, in 2002 Columbia House was reported to be merging with Blockbuster (which makes an appearance in Chapter 7). The merger never happened, but they eventually filed for bankruptcy in 2015. While the company still exists in a different capacity, I feel I outlasted my weakness.

The concept of an album club in the form of the old Columbia House is outdated. I don't think I'll have to worry about that pressure ever again. However, pressure still exists, and it's much different now. It's specifically acute in the music industry. It takes all of three seconds to click on a song and download it these days. You may not have to buy a whole album for $20, but you can easily buy thirty songs from a variety of artists for $1 apiece. The cumulative amount I would have paid for all the songs I acquired from Columbia house would have cost over $150. We didn't spend more than $50.

My intention is not to prevent you from listening to music, taking vacations, or participating in any recreation. It's to help you develop great decision-making habits that will sustain a positive, enjoyable relationship with money. You will refrain from playing long odds to satisfy money desires, and even the greatest Ponzi scheme will not be in the least bit enticing. You will learn to be consistent and to satisfy your short-term needs without sacrificing long-term stability. Most importantly, you will not have to rely on a quick buck.

Make the following things habitual and it will be much easier to rely on consistency and avoid the temptation to chase immediate success:

- Document your income.
- Track your spending.
- Prioritize saving and investing.

We have established the "get rich quick" plan is unwarranted. The next chapter will describe a sustainable, more recommended method for getting "rich."

Throughout the text, we will examine various topics in personal finance and explore how to address them in the modern world. We will identify consistent, positive behaviors that will help you manage your financial life. The information age has allowed us to gather rules, regulations, and strategies with ease, but how can we make wise decisions specific to our situation and not based on the social presentations we experience throughout the day?

4.

Break the Bank

HOW TO BECOME RICH, SLOWLY

What was the most memorable gift you received when you were a kid? Depending on your age, this could be something you've remembered for multiple decades. It had meaning in your life. It could have been a toy, a piece of clothing, or maybe a picture. Either way, you'll never forget it. It's likely there is some sort of lesson to learn.

It's interesting that sometimes the earliest lessons we learn are taken for granted. They have had the longest impact on our lives, but they've become so natural we don't even think about them.

Humans learn best through experience, and it's likely your most memorable gift includes some sort of event of which you were part. If we examine those times in our life, especially those from our early years, we often find the source of indelible lessons. Those lessons have been used to form great foundational habits and make good decisions for the balance of our life. It pays to review them on occasion and make sure they are not being taken for granted.

THE UNFORGETTABLE PIGGY

I received the most beautiful blue ceramic piggy bank when I was about eight years old. It taught me an extremely valuable lesson that sticks with me to this day.

"Out of sight, out of mind"

If you have children, you know a great way to make a child forget about something is to distract them with something else. Have you ever handed a toy to a kid who just fell? They were probably more startled than hurt, and hopefully the toy provided some joy to distract them from the fall.

My piggy bank was a great distraction. Every time I "fell" (got some coins), I would drop them in the bank. It sounded so rewarding when the coins hit the bottom of the fake ceramic hog. Ding-ding! I gathered up quite a bit of nickels and dimes from various sources.

Although not a traumatic experience like falling down for a kid, it was good for me to "forget" about my coins. There is something to be said for the rewarding experience of the noise the coins made when entering the bank. I wasn't putting money in the bank as a savings or budgeting practice.

I was an only child. It was more likely I would ask my parents to spend money on me than to save it. However, they must have understood I needed to experience something more than I needed to be told it.

After a period of about six months, I figured out my coins were adding up. I suddenly remembered many of the times I earned (or found) them. None of those times were extraordinary or unbelievable. It was mostly change from my parents checking out at the supermarket or finding a quarter on the ground somewhere. The piggy bank was running out of room, and I decided to try and open it.

Thankfully, the bank had one of those little plastic pieces at the opening, so you didn't have to actually break it to get the money out. It took a while to count the money, but it added up to about $50.

You might think I began to plan a spending spree, but I had no concept of money at eight years old. I didn't know how much anything was worth. I'm not sure if this was good or bad, but I didn't have any intention of spending the money. I was happier to be able to experience the "ding" of the coins hitting the bottom of the bank again.

I had a very simple desire: put coins in the bank. Listen to the "ding" and watch them pile up. I didn't know at the time, but the only line item I had was "savings." I can't stress the importance of that item. For the rest of my life, I've always made sure "savings" was prioritized in my budget. It's not whatever's leftover at the end of the month. It is the first "expense" that is covered in our household.

I'm not sure what happened to the blue piggy, but it served me really well. I learned small amounts of money add up over time. To this day, I always admire those big plastic soda bottle banks people fill up over a period of years or decades. That's dedication, and dedication is what every personal financial plan needs more than anything.

In this chapter, we will cover the foundational concept of personal finance, which requires great dedication. With the proper effort, you can identify what means the most to you, develop a plan, prioritize saving, and be confident in your success.

BALLIN' ON BUDGET, LITERALLY

One of my favorite football players to watch over the past decade has been Rob Gronkowski (Gronk). He won a Super Bowl with the Tampa Bay Buccaneers after spending a year in retirement. Previously, his entire career was with the New England Patriots. This guy is an incredible athlete. Plus, he's got a great first name. Granted, he's known for some antics off the field (never anything illegal), but on the field he is one of the most dominant players of his generation. You have to admire great success at that level. Everyone is a tremendous athlete. Dominating grown men is a feat that few accomplish consistently.

While I could comment on Gronk's prowess on the field for a whole book, perhaps his off-the-field accomplishments (not the antics) are even more impressive. It has been said he never spends his NFL salary. *What?* How does he pay the bills? His personality has led to plenty of endorsement deals that enable him to do this. However, his savings efforts should still be acknowledged. He's truly "ballin" and budgeting.

Gronk retired after the 2018 season, at which point it was calculated that he earned about $54 million as an NFL player. That's a pretty nice nest egg. It's impressive to save that money because he doesn't need it to live and could easily blow it on overindulgent luxuries. It takes strong will-power or some great habits to prevent oneself from using careless discretion. Granted, he has more leeway than most, but that might be a credit to his dedication no matter the amount of his income.

In a 2019 CNBC article, Gronk admitted to finally giving in to temptation in 2018. "I ain't gonna just save it all; I like to splurge a little bit," he said. "Splurging" can certainly be part of your budget. As I've mentioned, I encourage it. It's important to enjoy the things that bring you the most joy in life. As long as it's budgeted, you have a controlled amount and are less likely to seek joy from other things that aren't as satisfying. Gronk said that in the ninth year of his career. That's nine straight years of dedication to the primary focus of his budget. The average NFL player's career lasts less than three years. This gives Gronk and his league-mates a different incentive than most for saving for retirement. It's likely he'll be able to earn money other ways after retiring from the NFL again. I'm sure he did well during his first year-long foray into the "retired life," but football only lasts so long. He'll want to save up for when he quits for good.

BASIC LESSONS FROM A STAR ATHLETE

Gronk's type of budgeting is different than most, and it would be hard to outspend what he earns. However, there are some lessons to be learned from his foundational budgeting habits.

Most are familiar with the term "budget," or an estimate of the amount of money you make versus the amount you expend. I will stress that it is an estimate. It is rarely an exact calculation, but the more accurate, the better.

Spending less than you make is the basic premise of budgeting. It seems pretty simple, but that's not always the case. There are two main situations that lead many people to fall short of this simple goal:

- Their fixed expenses outweigh their income.
- They spend money on unnecessary things that raise their expenses above their income.

Budgeting applies to individuals, families, and businesses of all sizes and complexities. Those with the least stress around money (regardless of amount) are those whose budget estimates are most accurate and provide the most leeway. For example, if you know you take home $5,000 per month and your fixed expenses total $3,000, the way you plan the remaining $2,000 is critical. If you underestimate how much you spend on luxuries, you are likely to run over your budget. It would be wise to plan $1,500 of additional spending, leaving you with a $500 cushion in case something unexpected comes up or you can't control an urge for something.

WEIGHTLIFTING AND BUDGETING

Effective budgeting is an exercise of consistency and also relates to Gronk in another way. To perform as an NFL athlete, he had to keep himself in top physical condition. I spoke with Jess Bost, an Olympic style weightlifting champion, financial advisor, and CrossFit coach in Augusta, Georgia. She coaches people to financial and physical fitness and finds a strong correlation to the emotions of each.

In helping people with their budget, Bost recommends creating a system to avoid impulsive spending habits which really hinder long-term goals. She sets up a savings account for her clients that does not have a debit card and deposits money either directly from paychecks or from their checking account automatically into the savings account. This avoids the closing of a bad habit loop. Bost believes advertisers "position their intrigues on 'this is how you'll feel.'" If you have a debit card to use, you're likely to use it to satisfy your craving in search of the feeling that advertisers have presented. She creates an automatic piggy bank for her clients. The "ding' is seeing it grow after every paycheck.

In our conversation, Bost also explained the similarity between the emotions of her clients in each of her roles. Someone who is struggling to balance their budget is experiencing the same type of frustration of someone having trouble completing a workout. Mindfulness is extremely important. You must identify what financial or physical goals are most important and spend your time and effort concentrating on them. This allows you to believe you can be successful.

If you don't believe, it's very hard to allow enough time for success. Budgeting requires prioritizing your expenses and exercise requires picking the movements you want to train. Bost says it takes about a year for her financial clients to perfect their plan, and they only need to commit to that at first. Otherwise, things can get overwhelming.

WE CAN ALL BE ELITE BUDGETERS

Michael Jordan once said, "You have to expect things of yourself before you can do them." Bost also noted elite athletes spend 30–40 percent of their day dedicated to their craft. They have an established goal. It's much easier to make progress when you isolate the things that mean the most and concentrate on them consistently. This provides satisfaction as you make progress and eliminates the need for pleasure from alternate sources. If you set aside an amount of money each month for your favorite luxury, you're less likely to feel the need to buy something else because you've been satisfied.

Finally, the joy people experience when accomplishing something they originally thought was impossible in the financial and physical realms is also similar. It's even more satisfying than the quick dopamine hit of a social media "like" or an online purchase. It's the culmination of consistent hard work and should provide ample confidence to reach the next goal. Bost said it's important people feel good about what they have done. This is a more legitimate feeling than that which is elicited by the advertisers mentioned above.

Eight-year-old Bobby was a tremendous budgeter. He was dedicated (to putting all his coins in his piggy bank) and, most importantly, had no expenses. Most adults do not have the luxury of the latter. Generally, the more expenses you have, the more complex your budget will be, and the more dedication and mindfulness you will need. We'll cover the different types of expenses and how to categorize them later.

BUDGETING FOR TODAY'S AVERAGE PERSON

An overwhelming majority of us have more expenses than sources of income. It's the way most societies work. I believe it provides the illusion we are making more (not to mention taxes, a topic for later in the book, specifically Chapter 12) and spending less than we actually are.

In recent years, we have seen more ways for people to add additional sources of income. This can make your situation more complicated, but it's also nice to have the extra streams. About three years ago, my team and I began to work with two separate individuals. Each of them was having trouble balancing their budget. They were gainfully employed but didn't have the right systems in place to increase their savings and investments.

One of the people we were trying to help worked in audio and video production and had consistent work with a solid employer. In fact, there were even significant overtime opportunities that paid a higher wage. The other person was a ride-share driver. This profession allows you great flexibility, but there are no healthcare insurance benefits (covered in Chapter 11), and there must be people seeking a ride to earn money.

In assisting these individuals, I noticed it was very important to identify a purpose for the money you earn. It is hard to consistently cover your expenses and stay ahead of unexpected issues if you don't view your income as one tool. You might think the person who was in production (with higher earnings) could have avoided debt and built up their savings and investments more easily. However, this wasn't the case.

Higher overtime pay was an opportunity to spend on unneeded luxuries for the media production person. Whenever something unexpected happened (like a flat tire or broken refrigerator), it led to more debt. They were accustomed to making minimum payments on debt and not paying down the principal (strategies for debt repayment are covered in Chapter 10). Bad habits had formed.

Our driver, on the other hand, was determined to develop good habits. With our assistance, this person created a plan that would have them out of debt in one year. I say they created the plan because it is important to have ownership. We definitely advised, but it was the person who developed the plan that would work best for them.

We calculated the additional amount of money needed to pay off all credit cards, student loans, and build an emergency fund (Chapter 6 covers emergency funds in detail), and the additional amount of driving needed to earn the money. It would take a year to complete the process, and we used a budgeting app to track everything. The technology was immensely helpful because it provided results up to the minute and made progress easy to see. It was helpful in making calculations but was perhaps more helpful in generating a positive feedback loop. Every time the person was paid, they could see it in their account. Then, we could see a payment reduce the burden, and it turned into something that was a motivation to drive more and pay down the debt faster.

After a year had passed, we had one person with increasing debt and stress (even though they got a promotion!) and another person who put themselves in a much better position strictly by being a bit more conscious of where each dollar they earned went. They worked a bit more, but that was only to speed up the process.

The average person can benefit greatly from tracking their money and committing to a system. Gronk's thought process can work for you, too.

THE ILLUSION OF A SMALL EXPENSE

Smaller expenses can seem less burdensome, but the amount of money over budget doesn't correlate to the total amount. Simple math tells us four multiplied by $25 adds up to $100 but spending $25 four times doesn't seem to have the same effect on your wallet as the big $100 purchase. What if one of those $25 purchases was $25.50 (just an additional $.50)? You're then over budget. A $100.50 expense isn't any further over, but it might be easier to feel it. Tracking the total amount you spend can help you avoid the mirage of a bunch of "small buys."

To budget effectively and practice great financial habits, you have to properly identify your total income and total expenses. It's a little harder than simply breaking the bank when it's time to pay for something. The adult version of me has many more line items on his budget than "savings-blue piggy bank." You will need to take initial steps to organize all of your sources and expenditures. Then, you'll need the proper tools and an understanding of how to use them, so the management of your personal finances is simple and effective. In the coming chapter, we'll begin our exploration with the two main aspects of your cash flow—the key to balancing your budget.

5.

Get Paid

UNDERSTANDING EVERY DOLLAR OF YOUR INCOME AND EXPENSES

One of the best feelings in the world is to get rewarded for your work. We've already covered approval from other people on social media as a dopamine eliciting event. Another reward and dopamine trigger is getting paid. Everyone looks forward to payday. It's what you get after two weeks of hard work.

Imagine if you did *not* get your money on payday? In some ways, we don't get our money these days. Direct deposit has allowed us to send it to a banking institution of choice, but direct debit has also allowed us to send money out to various other organizations. Once again, things are simpler (you don't have to take a physical check or cash to the bank in person) but too easy. Automatically paying your bills is a great feature, but it's too easy to set up recurring payments for non-essential things. It's important to auto-pay *yourself* first.

This chapter will concentrate on treating your income as a tool to support your current lifestyle with an eye on your future. You must consider the value of payday beyond just that single day. It should really be pay-*life*.

EVERY DOLLAR HAS A PURPOSE

The base of your financial life is your income. You can't accomplish anything without it. A pyramid is an excellent illustration of personal finance. At the bottom of the pyramid is the foundation. It supports everything else. Your income is your financial foundation. Your expenses are layered on top. They form your cash flow.

I recommend you use zero-based budgeting, where every last dollar will have a place in the pyramid supported by your income, and your cash flow should be even (because every dollar has a purpose) in normal months. Chapter 4 described the importance of budgeting, and my blue piggy bank was a forced savings. In zero-based budgeting, savings is simply a line item on your budget. Your net worth, or the total of all you own minus anything you owe, will grow if paying off debt and investing are also their own items.

The percentage of your budget you allocate toward different items will change over time. As you pay off debt, you'll likely be able to save and invest more. If you take on some debt, you'll need to cut back on the other things. One example of a suggested budget split is the 50/20/30 rule where half of your spending goes toward living expenses, 20 percent toward savings and investments, and the final 30 percent toward things you want but don't necessarily need.

Erin Lowery says in her book *Broke Millennial*, "It's understanding money, not just having it, that equals empowerment. You right now have a choice; you either let money control and define your life, or you can control it." This chapter will highlight the most critical parts of controlling your money: income and expenses.

INCOME

Malcolm Gladwell claims in his book *Outliers* that you need to work at something for ten thousand hours to become an expert. That seems like it would take a terribly long time to reach that feat, but it's just five years of working forty-hour weeks. It makes me think everyone can master multiple things in their life. According to the Bureau of Labor Statistics, the average American will have twelve jobs during their lifetime. That means it would take sixty years (of forty-hour work weeks) to master twelve positions. Let's say someone works for fifty years and masters ten. That's still a lot. Gone are the days of working an entire career for one organization and retiring with a healthy pension (a guaranteed income source in retirement). It is more likely we will take on multiple jobs, and perhaps multiple roles at one company, in an effort to advance our career. We are capable of doing it according to Gladwell's premise.

It's safe to say most people will have many sources of income in their lives. In addition to different sources of income, there are also different types (I'll identify them from a tax perspective in this chapter and taxes are covered in detail in Chapter 12). Modern technology has allowed flexibility for even employed people to start a "side hustle," or a business on the side.

Entrepreneurship is more popular than ever before. A 2021 Smallbizgenius article by Dragomir Simovic stated there are 582 million entrepreneurs in the US alone. Surprisingly, *The New York Times* reported that during the COVID-19 pandemic in 2020 Americans started 4.4 million businesses, a 24 percent increase over 2019. There are numerous potential explanations for this, but it's clear entrepreneurship is on the rise. Technology certainly has a role. The internet is saturated with digital business owners claiming to live an incredible life of travel and remote work. While these things are possible, they are not guaranteed, and guaranteed income is the easiest part of a budget.

Even fifty years ago, it was just not reasonable to predict how one's life, employment, and income would play out over a lifetime. Even if you got to be exactly what you said when someone would ask what you wanted "to be when you grow up," there's no way you could predict your income and longevity accurately. It's more likely some combination of chance and preparation will lead you to an opportunity (or lack thereof) you couldn't predict.

I would have thought you were crazy if fifteen years ago you told me I was going to write a book about personal finance and digital technologies, but here we are. I've mastered finance according to Malcolm Gladwell, as much as I cringe at claiming the "master" title in an ever-changing environment. Mathematically, I've put in about 37,440 hours in the financial field. It seems impossible, but what was unexpected has provided me with income for much of my adult life.

Prior to my financial career, I expected to spend fifty years in sports radio.

It was 2009 and school was close to being out for the summer. An unexpected visitor arrived at Our Savior Lutheran Church and School, a small private school in Plantation, Florida. Security wasn't that intense at the time, and John Weibel walked into the office. He surprised the three ladies working that day as he walked into the small room with busy desks.

John greeted the ladies and asked, "Do ya'll know anyone who would want to work in finance?"

They shuttered in unison, "Uhh, no!"

He replied, "C'mon. Ya'll gotta know someone..."

Reluctantly, one lady spoke up and said, "Mrs. DePasquale's husband's a pretty nice guy." (What was she thinking?).

John took Mrs. DePasquale's phone number and called her as soon as he left the office. He left a nice message, but she couldn't answer because she was teaching. Later that day, she listened to the message from the strange number from somewhere in Central Florida. John was really nice and requested to speak with me (Mrs. DePasquale's husband). My wife alerted me to the call when she came home that day and urged me to be a nice guy and call him back. She recognized the company he represented because her family had a business relationship with them since she was a new-born baby.

I knew I had to call John back, but I was determined to make it as quick a phone call as possible. He was a nice guy, but I could tell he was ready to lay on the praise and possibilities pretty quick. I'll never know exactly why, but for some reason I told him I'd call him back in six months. I assume it was just to get him off the phone.

Six months went by and I had a couple of days off during the holiday season. This was rare in my radio career. I thought of my conversation with John. My parents raised me to be a man of my word. I had to follow through on my promise. Somehow, I found his number and I called him back. He answered and was surprised someone would actually reach out after that much time. It took a minute to recognize who I was, but he quickly picked up where he had left off. We met a couple of times for him to wine and dine my wife and me. I'd be lying if I didn't acknowledge that I probably didn't need two nice dinners to be convinced to make the move at that point. The radio conglomerate I was working for had participated in some morally questionable practices and it made me feel uncomfortable.

Before you knew it, I was a new financial representative. It was a rather nebulous title, but it had a nice ring. There were a lot of new things about the career. I was no longer talking into a microphone. I had to speak directly to people. Math, over writing, was a foundational skill. Advertisers were no longer in control; I was. The thing that stuck out the most about the new life was the income. It was variable and from multiple sources. I was no longer guaranteed a paycheck, and when I was to get paid, it could be from any of five different entities. This was a challenge, especially when working on my income taxes. I needed to understand how I was compensated.

I was paid mostly on a commission basis. My employer paid me to sell their products and services. The more I sold, the more I would make. Many people in commissionable jobs prefer the unlimited upside of their income. They can work as much as they want to make as much as they want. I have found this often sounds much better than it is. It takes great discipline to limit your time "on the job" when money dominates your sense of purpose.

I worked hard on making sure I had time for family and mental relaxation, but it was not easy. My employer celebrated those with the highest numbers, and it was natural to chase different financial metrics. With that being said, if I didn't work, my variable income would vary downward. Contributing to the complexity was the legal formation of the company for which I worked. I had multiple paychecks from different legal companies. Budgeting was a disaster.

I had to learn the importance of reserves, which is covered more in the next chapter. It was imperative to plan for an inconsistent paycheck. It took years, but I eventually built up a fund that had enough money to cover all our expenses for at least six months. If I had a slow month at work, I couldn't succumb to any well-placed targeting ads. Once the reserves were accessed, the rule was they must be replenished before participating in other unscheduled spending.

Once I was able to solidify my income and reserves situation, it comfortably supported my family for twelve years. This is longer than the 4.1 years the Bureau of Labor Statistics (2020) stated as the average time a worker was with their current employer. It was still an unpredictable change at the time I took the job, and it functioned as multiple sources of income.

I advocate for people to spend their ten thousand hours honing their skills. It makes it easier for the rest of us to find an expert in the field they need. I also understand the ease at which people switch careers and positions, the competitive recruitment industry, and the numerous sources of income people desire. Therefore, it's imperative to have a solid understanding of how your income is structured.

A clear understanding of your income structure strengthens the foundation of your financial pyramid. This is important because you cannot pay expenses without it, and it will define many of your life decisions. As mentioned, many entrepreneurs will tell you it's best to have multiple streams of income. It will raise the amount (assuming it doesn't limit your original sources) and spread-out risk. Yet, it's more complex.

There are three main types of income:

1. Earned Income—money you receive by working, i.e., your salary.
2. Passive Income—money you receive without working, i.e., interest on your bank account.
3. Capital Gains—money you receive from a sale, i.e., selling a stock for more than you purchased it.

Each of these categories has subsets but the most important thing is that you know all the places you consistently receive money from and the amounts. The more accurate your projections are, the better. It's much easier to budget for a salaried job than an unpredictable, commission-based position. For many, their job is the only reasonably predictable source of income, and the others are either insignificant or not consistent enough to include in a budget.

Sort your sources of income to reasonably predict what your total will be in a given period.

NON-DISCRETIONARY EXPENSES

Discretion is the freedom to decide what should be done in a given situation. In budgeting, some things allow for discretion and others do not. This is a very important part of forming your budget. The United States gross domestic product (GDP) in 2019 was $21.43 trillion dollars. This is a measure of the value of the goods and services produced within the country. Our monetary system and economy are explained more closely in Chapter 9, but understanding spending is essential for this section of the book.

Seventy percent of GDP was from consumer spending. That's about $15 trillion spent on personal use and enjoyment. While this is a driving force of the economy, I believe we could stand to monitor our consumption a little bit more closely. The average person spends about $18,000 per year on nonessential items, and the average salary is around $50,000. That means we spend almost 40 percent of what we earn on things we could go without. Think about what else could be done with that money. What if the number was closer to the 50/20/30 rule's 30 percent on wants?

Everyone understands the importance of eating and having a dwelling. They make for an easy understanding of things for which we must budget.

There are some restrictive diets out there. Try intermittent fasting, but you still have to spend money on some sort of food. I also know some people who live in an RV year-round. They may not have a single-family home or apartment to pay for, but an RV carries a significant expense.

It's possible to avoid paying for a traditional diet and house, but we all have to sustain life. You're going to have to eat at some point and an RV is not free to operate. These are not discretionary because you must have them.

Non-discretionary expenses are costs you know you will incur and have no choice to eliminate (i.e., your rent). They must be considered in your budget, and many will never go away. They are things that are either required to sustain life or things to which you have committed. Some examples are:

- food
- mortgage
- rent
- utilities
- car loan

Some non-discretionary expenses are easier to budget for than others because they are fixed amounts. Your rent or mortgage payment is not likely to change in amount frequently, whereas your utility bill is not fixed and can depend on the season of the year. However, you should be able to budget a reasonably accurate amount based on experience.

DISCRETIONARY EXPENSES

In keeping with the eating and dwelling examples, let's consider items with which we have a choice. On the other end of the diet spectrum is a great night out at a fancy restaurant. There's also a big family vacation that might involve an RV. These things aren't necessary to life, but they may be really important to you.

Discretionary expenses (wants) are not needed. They might be related to special occasions, or they might just be things you couldn't imagine going without. In some cases, you might move them into the non-discretionary category because they're that important to you. Here are some examples:

- cell phone
- cable TV/streaming
- other entertainment subscriptions
- internet
- vacations
- dining out
- video games

This is certainly not an exhaustive list. There are endless things you can spend your money on, and these are where the majority of impulse buying would land. I find things in this category, especially the non-fixed items, are the most important to keep track of due to their unpredictable nature. It's easy enough to consider your static internet bill every month, but something like dining out tends to be more unpredictable. You get home late from work and don't feel like cooking, so you decide what restaurant to go to while in the car without consulting the budget and considering the exact price. You might also catch an enticing luxury while scrolling Amazon and buy it with "1-click." These things are acceptable, as long as you have budgeted space for discretionary purchases. If you've spent that allocation, you must be disciplined enough to wait until the following month.

PUBLIC TOOLS FOR PERSONAL SUCCESS

There are many tools to help you manage your cash flow and keep a strong budget (especially one that is zero-based). Some are technologically advanced, while others are much older methods, but just as effective. A corded telephone is not useless because of the sound quality. It's the extra expense that has led many to hold just a cellular line. Fortunately, most budgeting tools don't come at a monetary cost.

WRITTEN LEDGER

The old-fashioned pen and paper are surprisingly effective because they enable you to visualize your situation every time you make calculations. I suggest using a monthly time frame, as many sources of income and expenses use this period.

Start by writing down your sources of income. Add up the monthly amounts. Then do the same for your non-discretionary expenses. Subtract the expenses from the income. Hopefully, you have a positive number.

The amount you come up with is the amount of money you have in surplus to spend on discretionary expenses and save monthly. Don't skip saving.

Income:
Salary—$4,000/month

Non-Discretionary Expenses:
Rent—$2,000/month
Utilities—$200/month
Car loan—$250/month
Cell Phone—$50/month
Streaming—$50/month
Internet—$50/month
Food—$250/month

Total—$2,850

Discretionary Expenses:
Entertainment—$100/month
Dining Out—$100/month
Vacation Fund—$100/month

Total—$300/month

$4,000 - ($2,850+$300) = $850/month—You have $850/month left over. Save it.

ENVELOPE SYSTEM

Another method is called the envelope system. Here, you put actual cash in separate envelopes. It provides a hard limit to your spending. If you only put $100 in your discretionary (wants) envelope, once that $100 is gone for the month, then that's it. If you spend $100 on a night out the first weekend of the month, then you'll be hanging out at home the next few weeks. You *cannot* dip into your $850 savings envelope to supplement. It's ideal to keep this money out of an easily accessible envelope. We'll cover interest and investing later, but those provide additional reasons to keep your savings out of reach.

You may not want to handle cash in envelopes, but you can create this system digitally if it's easier but just as effective for you. Most banks have apps and other software that will create different "envelopes" or accounts for each category.

You'll have a little math or examining to do each month no matter which system you use. There are plenty of applications that will help you budget. Your needs determine which is best.

It's most important that you work toward having a surplus every month. If and when you have that surplus, it needs to be put in the proper place. It is *not* appropriate to put it in your ceramic piggy bank. The surplus is still part of the zero-based budget as it is earmarked to pay off debt, save for emergencies, and invest for the future. You don't want the debt to balloon, an emergency to ruin the budget you worked hard to perfect, or a lack of growth to put your purchasing power and future budget at risk.

Some helpful personal financial management applications include:

Mint: a popular, longstanding program that aggregates accounts, categorizes, and provides alerts to keep you on budget

Mvelopes: digital envelopes

Good Budget: an envelope system for couples

You Need a Budget: "$0 Budgeting" that gives every $1 a role, preventing unnecessary spending

BUDGT: an iPhone-only app focusing on daily tracking

Wally: a free app focusing on tracking expenses

Pocketguard: an app that is easy to use, links accounts, provides suggestions on lowering expenses, provides cash flow projections

All of these are great tools to help you make wise financial decisions. Budgeting apps are not exciting to talk about, but they can save you lots of money if used consistently.

You can use their features to put psychology on your side. It feels good to fill up an "envelope" earmarked for your family vacation. It also feels good when you are "green" at the end of the month. This is how modern technology is good for your personal finances.

Use today's technology to execute the foundational habits of budgeting, use your income as wisely as possible, and pay yourself. You might "get paid" by your employer but is some of that money ultimately benefiting you in the long term? Your digital adult piggy bank could be the single most important part of your finances. It's not flashy and it's not what most finance experts talk about, but it's the first thing you need to master related to your money, and the sooner you do the more you'll benefit. Everything else in your pyramid, no matter how advanced, relies on a well-balanced budget.

6.

Straight Cash

———

SECURING WHAT YOU'VE EARNED

What should your financial plan have in common with a sandcastle? More than you might think.

I've spent many years with families dreaming of their life and financial goals. I estimate I've worked on two thousand projects. The most meaningful ones are those in which people commit to making major changes to their financial habits. The most disappointing are either those that have a major disruption or those that ended completely.

There is no avoiding certain financial catastrophes such as death or destructive weather (hurricanes, floods, etc.). There are also certain measures that should be taken to mitigate risks as much as possible.

Completing visioning exercises is similar to building a sandcastle. It can be a fun and rather extravagant undertaking. You can build whatever you want, and there is really no true risk. The stakes in your goal setting or beach day are nothing, unless you're part of one of the many sand sculpture tournaments across the world. In my research for this text, I couldn't help but look into the competitive sandcastle landscape. I was surprised by what I found. Some of the competitions draw thousands of views and might have fifty teams on a beach at a single time.

What a shame it would be if the world's largest sandcastle in Copenhagen, Denmark fell because of a stiff breeze or high tide. The massive sculpture stands 69.4 ft (21.16 m) and weighs nearly five thousand tons. I wouldn't want to be observing closely if that thing toppled. I am sure there are plenty of safety measures put in place to keep it standing.

Just like the Guinness World Record-holding sandcastle, you should put things in place to prevent your financial life from falling over. We will cover some more advanced protection concepts in Chapter 11. For now, we need to make sure the base of our financial house is protected.

PROTECTING WHAT YOU'VE EARNED

The next most important thing after securing your budget is making sure it doesn't become insecure. You need to protect against unexpected expenses. It would be a shame to do a lot of work on it only to have one event ruin everything and cause you financial hardship. The premise applies to budgets of all sizes, individuals, families, and organizations.

The Great Recession (December 2007 to June 2009) is widely considered the worst economic situation since the Great Depression of the 1930s. The causes of the event in the '30s are still debated to this day. A stock market crash, international trade issues, and excessive production have all been blamed. Monetary policy, the money supply, and ultimately the Federal Reserve (which is examined in detail in Chapter 9) seem to be the most at fault. Still, it's not clear if the situation could have been avoided.

The situation in the late 2000s was different. It may be because it's more recent history or maybe information technology is more reliable, but the causes are a little clearer, and it was reported by a special government-organized commission as avoidable. In its 2011 report, its purpose is described as so, "The Financial Crisis Inquiry Commission was created to 'examine the causes of the current financial and economic crisis in the United States.'" It was clear that there was a crisis, but it was hard to isolate a single cause. The report also stated, "The profound events of 2007 and 2008 were neither bumps in the road nor an accentuated dip in the financial and business cycles we have come to expect in a free market economic system. This was a fundamental disruption—a financial upheaval if you will—that wreaked havoc in communities and neighborhoods across this country." It was a prolonged significant issue and something that was systemic. It was not a quick downturn and it didn't have to be that bad. The first conclusion listed by the commission in its report explicitly expressed this:

"We conclude this financial crisis was avoidable. The crisis was the result of human action and inaction, not of Mother Nature or computer models gone haywire. The captains of finance and the public stewards of our financial system ignored warnings and failed to question, understand, and manage

evolving risks within a system essential to the well-being of the American public."

Coming out of the 2001 ".com Bubble," the Federal Reserve lowered interest rates significantly. In addition, there were favorable federal policies related to homeownership. It was easy to obtain loans, and people were encouraged to buy homes. Adjustable-rate mortgages and other exotic forms of financing lead to heavy reliance on interest rates moving forward. The Federal Reserve raised interest rates higher and faster than expected to stay in line with target inflation rates. Adjustable-rate mortgages adjusted way higher than expected and default rates spiked. Home values tanked and the housing "bubble" burst. Certain investments tied to home loans, such as mortgage-backed securities, which had been sold aggressively, took a deep drop in value.

The banks that financed the housing boom were over-leveraged and many collapsed. Most famous of these banks was Bear Stearns. In March of 2008, the Federal Reserve approved a $30 billion bailout to save the bank. At the end of the 2007 fiscal year, it had reported a leverage ratio of 35.6 to 1 (compared to 5.25 the previous year), meaning it had a very low amount of capital compared to its assets. It was holding far too much debt.

Some of the largest banks in the world failed because they weren't prepared for an emergency. They had no safety net and were bound to collapse if there was a major issue. There are regulations in place now to prevent this sort of thing from happening again.

More information on the Great Recession can be found in the Financial Crisis Inquiry Commission at fcic.gov.

If massive investment banks need rules to prevent failure in case of a catastrophe, so does your financial plan. Don't rely on your own $30 million bailout. It's not coming. US citizens could have received up to $1,400 ($2,800 for married couples) from a third pandemic-related stimulus in 2021, but this is related to a macroeconomic situation, not your personal budget.

There are plenty of rules to prevent fraud, but you are going to have to make your own rules to prevent bankruptcy. You'll need to have a significant amount of capital in case of emergency, and you'll want to know the best place to put it. It is up to you to put rules in place to create your own personal bailout. The good news is with the proper planning, executing it is far less complicated than that of Bear Stearns. It's simple: you need "straight cash."

EMERGENCY FUND, SAVINGS, AND INTEREST

One thing eight-year-old Bobby didn't get from his piggy bank was interest. As great as the story might be, there's a better place to put your money than a piggy bank. A deposit institution like a bank or credit union is designed to hold your money, keep it safe, and usually provides some form of interest to you to store your money with them. That's right, they pay you so they can hold the money. They do this because they use that money to lend to others and make more money. This arrangement makes sense for individuals because they can earn some interest while having liquidity (ability to access the money quickly) and limited risk. The Federal Deposit Insurance Corporation (FDIC) insures up to $250,000 per depositor, per institution, for each type of account. See fdic.gov for more information. It would not make sense for an individual to be loaning money out to others because there is no guarantee they get it back, and there's a chance they would not be able to access it when needed.

You should be commended for managing your budget and giving yourself a margin for error. What are you supposed to do with that $850 (from the Chapter 5 example) surplus you have every month? You know you shouldn't spend it. You need to save it, and you need it to multiply.

The first place for your $850 to go is your emergency fund (your "straight cash"). Take a look at your budget and identify the amount of your monthly expenses. If there was an emergency and you could no longer earn money, how would you pay those expenses? You could cut out all the discretionary ones, but you would still need to pay the non-discretionary bills. The emergency fund allows you to if you stop earning money. Most experts will recommend you have three to six months of expenses saved there.

Sticking with the previous example, your emergency fund should have between $8,550 (3 months) and $17,100 (6 months). The more consistent your income, the more you can skew toward three months. If you are paid strictly on commission, you'll want to have more because you are not guaranteed to get paid.

Your Emergency Fund must be invested in an account that has very limited or no restrictions to getting the money. This type of account is described as "liquid." A good place is a checking or savings account at your bank or credit union. Savings accounts generally earn you more but may limit the number of times you can take money out in a given period. It's not likely you'll need frequent withdrawals from the account, but make sure you can get to it immediately in case of emergency.

With your deposit, an institution will offer you a percentage of earnings on your money called an Annual Percentage Yield (APY).

If you deposit $100 in a bank and they offer you a .5 percent APY, you'll make $.50 if you kept the $100 in for the entire year. In actuality, you'd earn more than that because the rate would compound interest each time interest is credited (usually more than yearly), but the APY is an easy way to understand what the institution is offering.

Some good websites to visit for shopping interest rates are bankrate.com, depositaccounts.com, and magnifymoney. com. This is a great use of technology to aggregate information and update rates daily, but you should be aware the institutions pay as advertisers to be part of the site. So once again, advertisers are influencing what you see.

ALTERNATIVE FINANCIAL SERVICES

Not everyone has a bank, unfortunately. Some people are missing out on checking and savings accounts for the interest they provide, the ease of use, and the $250,000 of FDIC protection.

Tyrone Ross is the CEO of Onramp Invest. Onramp is a digital native investment platform for the next generation advisor.

Ross grew up in what he would describe as an underserved home. His family often relied on money orders and sometimes even scratch-off lottery tickets to cover their budget. A bank wasn't an option to keep their funds because of lack of access and other preventative things like low-balance fees. Families in these situations often develop a distrust for deposit institutions because they become accustomed to being denied loans and products and incurring unexpected charges.

Ross' family needed access to money immediately and technology of the time didn't allow them to get their money right away. In this environment, none of the advantages of having a bank could be used and they were forced to use other methods. They relied on cash. These days, some places refuse to even accept cash. Not having a bank is a problem.

In addition to not having the benefits of a deposit institution, those who are without one don't learn how to use the tools that many take for granted. If you never had to write out a check, how would you know how to? It's just easier to use a money order and have it done for you. Unfortunately, the issue is not that clear. Ross admitted, "I didn't realize it's a bigger problem until I got into financial services."

THE UNLIKELY FINANCIAL THOUGHT LEADER

Ross' journey to his current role is truly amazing. The financial services industry is a competitive world, and he started at a distinct disadvantage. In fact, he was actually a corrections officer prior to his financial career. He has said, "There's no direct route to Wall Street if you grew up in a home that was completely unbanked."

Ross' mother would boil water to create heat when they were cold. His father couldn't read or write, and Tyrone was the first in his family to graduate high school. Hard work earned him a track scholarship to Georgia Tech University where he would study biomedical engineering, but he was kicked out twice. He got his associate degree at community college and enrolled in Seton Hall University. Ineligibility to run because of National Collegiate Athletic Association Rules led him to spend a little more time on schoolwork when he first joined his new school. He earned academic honors and competed in his senior season on the track.

Two years after school (2004), he tried to make the US Olympic Trials. He failed. A couple of years later, he unexpectedly started a career on Wall Street and tried to work and train for the 2008 Olympics. Unfortunately, he missed the time he needed to qualify by a half of a second. He was twenty-eight years old and passed his prime as a runner, but he decided to continue.

In 2012 (the next Olympic year) while training, his grandmother died, his best friend committed suicide, he suffered a complete groin tear, and he was fired from Morgan Stanley. One morning, he was on a run and nearly jumped in front of a truck. It seemed as if all the success he had was non-existent. He was a tremendous athlete but injured; a previously successful financial consultant but broke. It was a dark time. The Olympics, again, were out of the question.

Ross had been "living his life for his resume." Now, he "lives it for his legacy."

Tyrone's money experience was a struggle growing up, and he did not take any business or finance courses in college. Yet, a professor of his encouraged him to seek a job on Wall Street. After some experience, he had a mentor at Lehman Brothers who recommended he start to work directly with investors on the retail side of the business. This was a good fit with his ability to develop relationships. Eventually, he landed a job at Merrill Lynch after his boss that fired him from Morgan Stanley got him an interview (that didn't go well). He overcame again and was determined to outwork everyone else.

The story is incredible. It illustrates the struggle lack of financial services can lead to, but also shows how it can be changed. Tyrone was named on the Invest News 40 under 40 list despite not knowing what a stock was until he was twenty-six!

Ross's position as CEO of a technologically advanced cryptocurrency firm does not point to his early experiences with money, but it is still relevant. It just needs to be applied to the digital age. He said he now hopes to take the educational and availability principles of his situation growing up and apply them to today's world.

Banking is now done mostly digitally. You can pay for things and deposit checks using your mobile phone. Financial literacy is the ability to understand and use various financial skills. This includes budgeting and digital literacy. We'll cover it more in Chapter 16. People need to understand how to use and be comfortable using electronic devices to run their budgets. The tools are great if you can.

A 2019 Federal Reserve Study stated 77 percent of American adults were "fully banked." This means they have a relationship with a bank or credit union and don't rely on alternative services. The remaining 23 percent of Americans (almost 75.5 million) rely on alternative services, such as payday loans and money orders, completely or at least in part (see Chapter 10 for a detailed description of these vehicles). That is a large portion of a big country.

The expense payday loans, money orders, and check cashing transactions incur is a terrible drag on a budget. They provide access to cash quickly, and fees are generally very transparent but quoted over a much shorter time frame than bank products. They can seem easier to understand than their bank-style counterparts, but repeated use is shown to cost more when compared to holding a bank product over a similar period of time. Although, if your rent is due and you don't get paid until the next week, you may need a payday loan to cover you until then.

According to the FDIC, four of the top five reasons people don't deal with banks is because they don't trust them, the fees are too high, the fees are not transparent, and avoiding the bank provides privacy.

There is certainly a trust issue. Privacy is clearly important, and while the digitization of finance is designed to be safe, there is a concern. People should feel comfortable their hard-earned money is safe. An emergency fund doesn't serve its purpose if you're not sure it will be around. We need to provide access and peace of mind to the underserved.

On a positive note, the FDIC also reported the completely unbanked percentage of Americans moved down to 5.4 percent in 2019 from 6.5 percent in 2017. This is a good sign, but there is still work to do.

THE UNDERSERVED

Ross believes the term unbanked is a trope because it doesn't "go to the scope of the problem." He said, "underserved" is probably a better term and "to be unbanked is just a small part of what it means to be underserved." More than a depository institution is needed. There needs to be adequate financial education and opportunities to avoid the shortcomings of alternative financial services.

Technology has added to the ease of banking (for those who are comfortable using devices) and things should continue to improve. The lesson is it can be challenging to apply the foundational steps of a budget without the proper support. As things advance, we need to keep everyone up to date on how to use what is available.

Regardless of the exact types of accounts and institutions you use, it's of utmost importance you protect your finances in case of emergency. Your emergency fund is like a sea wall in front of the most important sandcastle you ever built. It's not the most exciting place to put your money that you might see on your social feed, but you have to keep a designated cash stash that's easy to access and earns a guaranteed fixed interest rate. This is your safety net. With it in place, you could be more solvent than a multi-trillion-dollar investment bank that gets caught up in the newest overhyped investment.

7.

Money Talks

———

THE STORY YOUR INVESTMENTS TELL

Imagine if you were a master sand sculpture craftsman. You would probably feel comfortable in ensuring your sandcastles aren't swept away by a wave or blown over by a stiff wind. There are no guarantees, but your confidence that the base of your creation is safe would give you some leeway to add some more extravagant features. It would be acceptable to take some risks to improve a sculpture. However, you still need to be careful to make sure your castle in the sand doesn't topple over. No risk should be extreme enough to ruin everything.

It's a great feeling when you've established a solid emergency fund. You are earning money on your money because even an emergency fund can earn a little bit of interest in a savings account. There's a sense of safety and accomplishment. There can also be a sense of relief, but you can't rest on those self-provided laurels. You must continue to execute your plan and keep your budget intact so as to not backslide. Thankfully, modern technology has made keeping track of things a bit easier. Continue to make it work for you.

If you've had debt or other expenses that had previously prevented you from building your savings, you have somewhat of a head start in the next steps. You have "free money" in your budget to put toward your future. The hard decisions will be where to put it and what to invest in.

IMPULSIVE OR JUST CURRENT?

In my years working with families and their finances, I learned current events have a massive influence on decision-making. Elections, governmental policy changes, stock market fluctuations, health and safety items like a pandemic or terrorist attack, and even sports news tend to trigger decision patterns. They are not necessarily good or bad, but the things we see and hear about the most tend to stay top of mind when we determine what we are going to do in a given situation with their consideration. Money is certainly not exempt from this concept. Technology and social media have only accelerated this process. We experience things faster than ever before.

If you see an article or ad about a new electronic device, it's likely you have shown interest in that type of item before. You might spend a surplus in your budget on that item. The social media algorithm worked. You might also see a snippet of a concert that your favorite music artist recently performed. Maybe you'd purchase a song or look for tickets the next time the artist is performing locally. These decisions are not terrible for a financial plan, but repeated impulse purchases could be. It's best to direct all or at least the majority of your surplus toward long-term growth. It should be part of the budget to contribute to your financial future. This is a foundation of zero-based budgeting.

Aside from impulse purchases, there are other decisions of where to put your money. Most would agree investing is a smart practice for financial wealth building. However, it must be done wisely. The same principles of impulsive consumption can also apply here. Suppose you hear about a hot new investment at the water cooler at work? Or you catch an interesting Twitter thread about it? You could think to yourself that buying some of that company is an advisable long-term financial decision. It might be, but it might also be a dopamine-seeking, crowd-chasing move. This would be speculating. The hot new buy could be more of a backslide than even the most indulgent of consumptive purchases. Don't collapse the sandcastle with a single risk.

SPECULATING

You should continue to identify risk and save money when your emergency fund is full, but you can do it in a different fashion. Risk can now be accepted, yet it should be mitigated. You are ready to invest—not speculate.

A complete examination of all investment options and strategies is well beyond the scope of this text, but it's important to understand how investing fits into one's finances.

The stock market tends to get quite a bit of publication. Unfortunately, it's often for the wrong reasons. When you purchase a stock, you are investing directly into a company. You are supporting what it supports. You are predicting it will be successful. Most investors operate in this manner. Some, however, bet on a stock losing value, which is called short selling.

Short selling was a popular topic early in 2021 when a large group of motivated retail investors decided to purchase large amounts of shares of the company GameStop.

The news aggregation and discussion website Reddit has what are called "subreddits." These are communities that have isolated a specific topic. One subreddit is known as Wall Street Bets. This particular group is known for its aggressive trading strategies.

There is nothing out of the ordinary with aggressive trading, but in one instance their motives were not due to confidence in the company they purchased. They were actually attacking much wealthier investors by creating what is called a "short squeeze."

On January 13, 2021, GameStop's stock price climbed 57.9 percent from $19.95 to $31.40. That's an incredible day. Over the next two weeks, the stock climbed to unprecedented heights. On the 27th, it was $347.51, which was 134.84 percent higher than the previous day and almost 17.5 times the stock price just two weeks prior.

GameStop is a brick-and-mortar video game retailer with a business model that is being replaced by online gaming sites like Steem. People are just not shopping in person for video games. Some compare it to Blockbuster Video (a video rental company) being overtaken by downloading and streaming video services. Its long-term viability is questioned by many. There was no traditional reasoning for so many people investing in it and its price to spike so high, so rapidly.

The Wall Street Bets community caused the price of the stock to rise so much that many "expert" hedge fund investors were forced to come up with shares of a stock that they expected to go down. These organizations sell a company like GameStop short by borrowing shares of it through their broker, selling them at the current price, and hoping it will lose value. When it goes down, they buy the stock back for a lesser amount and give it back to whoever they bought it from.

If the price of a "shorted" stock rises, short-sellers are forced to buy back the shares they borrowed to cut their losses and cover themselves as the price continues to rise. This causes a cascading effect that can put the whole system in a bind. In this case, more shares of GameStop were shorted than were outstanding, and investors were scrambling to buy shares as the demand exceeded the supply. It forced many brokerage firms to halt trading and led to numerous other issues.

By the time the price reached its height, many speculators outside of Wall Street Bets were involved. On the 28th, the stock dropped 44.29 percent. The next day it spiked again (67.87 percent) as day traders had joined the party. Some people made quite a bit of money and some lost even more. It was a hectic week on Wall Street, to say the least.

Hedge funds are investment companies that pool resources from wealthy investors and use very sophisticated strategies to earn returns and mitigate risks. The people who run them are considered very experienced investors. It's ironic a Reddit community could "take down" the big guys.

This event was certainly not a long-term gradual growth strategy. It was some combination of a "quick-buck" and "Davids vs. Goliaths." Ultimately, some were successful in making some quick money. More importantly, they highlighted some of the problems with the system and illustrated that modern technology has a major effect on our world. None of this would have happened without the internet. That doesn't mean short squeezes are bad or should never happen. In fact, it's happened plenty of times, including a few in the last decade, but those events weren't incited in the same fashion.

It's sad that something like this and the lawsuits that followed had to happen, but when information travels so quickly, things can happen unexpectedly. You have to understand the digital age pumps up the popularity of get-rich-quick opportunities. In my conversation with Jess Bost that I outlined in Chapter 4, she mentioned the most frequent questions she gets from her clients are about popular news stories like the GameStop saga because they feel they are going to miss out. Unfortunately, she says, "The social media world stimulates this idea that you could win big." It makes people look to play catch-up as they feel they are behind.

Morgan Housel, who I first referenced in Chapter 3, provides an excellent point: "We think about and are taught about money in ways that are too much like physics (with rules and laws) and not enough like psychology (with emotions and nuance)." This is not to say we should make emotional decisions with our investments. It means we must understand that psychology plays a role, and decisions should not be based solely on facts and figures shared through social media or any other type of media.

INVESTING

It would have been nice to quadruple (or more) your money in a short squeeze, but this is not a sustainable investment model. It's not the way to save for retirement or any other long-term goal. It's not saving.

Housel also says, "Rationale optimism most of the time masks the odds of ruin some of the time. The result is we systematically underestimate risk." This means we usually have a reasonable belief in success, but it makes us overlook the risks that will cause troubles occasionally. Even though we want to make a lot of money in a short period of time, we generally understand we are not likely to. However, we don't generally acknowledge the severity of the risks we are subject to. Investing, whether rational or not, always involves risk. It should be done systematically.

There are multiple calculations and benchmarks for how much money you should be saving. Many say it's somewhere around 15 percent of your income. Each person's situation is different, and I don't believe a general rule is appropriate. What's most important is being able to consider how much money you will need at a given time (in most cases retirement) and then being able to project out how much you'll earn in the years leading up to the date.

For example, if you believe you can live off of $1,000,000 at age seventy, and you are age thirty now, you have forty years to get there. If you have no savings now, you'll need to contribute $13,000 per year, assuming you earn 6 percent returns every year. That's a fairly conservative long-term earnings rate, but it's better to be conservative than to overestimate and come up short.

Age: 30
Retirement Age: 70
Yearly Savings: $13,000/year
Average Yearly Earnings Rate: 6 percent
Goal: $1,000,0000

If you earned 4 percent yearly on your $1,000,000 in retirement, you would generate $40,000 per year. If that, combined with any other sources of income is sufficient, great. If it's not, you'll either be eating into the $1,000,000 every year, or you'll need to make some adjustments to your savings or earnings rate (during working years or in retirement). You can improve your savings rate by adjusting your budget, but you can only attempt to improve the earnings rate.

It's best to maintain your principal amount so you always have sufficient income.

Savings Amount at Retirement (Age 70): $1,000,000
Yearly Earnings Rate: 4 percent
Income Generated per Year without using principal: $40,000
Length of Income: as long as needed
Savings Amount at Age 100: $1,000,000

It would be better to try to earn more in your younger years because you'll need to take additional risk and, as Housel warns, you need to be aware of that.

Investing carries a risk-reward tradeoff. Generally, the more risk you take, the higher returns possible and vice versa. Seeking higher returns is more advisable when you are younger because you have more time to offset potential losses experienced from the additional risk.

Technology allows you to execute many of the basic premises of investing, including managing your risk, with ease. There are questionnaires that help determine how many risks you are comfortable with, and there is software that evaluates the risk being taken in a given portfolio. Technology also helps with diversification, which is the concept of spreading your investments across many different options.

A portfolio highly concentrated in one position is unnecessarily subject to the risks and volatility of that one investment. Investments such as mutual funds and exchange traded funds allow you to invest in hundreds of companies at once. Technology also allows you to quickly make projections and see how the time value of money is working for you. The longer you have, the more time your returns have to compound.

As much as technology helps, it also gives us access to other strategies that require a sophistication that most do not have the time or expertise to execute.

TYPES OF INVESTMENTS

Companies like Robinhood (which was heavily publicized in the GameStop short squeeze) and E-Trade have well-developed mobile applications that provide access to stocks, bonds, mutual funds, index funds, bond funds, exchange-traded funds, derivatives, and margin accounts, amongst other investments. Each of these carries their own level of sophistication, different rules, and unique purposes. While they make access to these investments easier, they do not provide people with the experience and education needed to be good traders. In fact, previous evidence suggests many of the people who use these services underperform the market as a whole.

One of my favorite investment premises comes from Dr. Daniel Crosby. He referenced his "10 Commandments for Investor Behavior" on *The Long View* podcast and said, "If you're excited about it, it's probably a bad idea."

Up until August of 2020, Robinhood provided "popularity data" that allowed you to see the performance of its investors as a whole (about thirteen million people in May 2020, shortly after the GameStop incident from above). A site called Robintrack used to follow and report the data. In the two years prior to its shutdown, it reported Robinhood users average 6.2 percent less annualized returns than the S & P 500 (an index of the 500 largest publicly-traded companies in the United States). It appears it would have been simpler and better to passively invest your money across hundreds of companies.

Stocks, like the shares in the GameStop situation, are a share of ownership of a company. When you own stock in a company, you actually own a portion of the it.

Stocks come in two different forms: common and preferred. Common stocks are more readily available and come with voting rights and equity ownership. Preferred stocks have some priorities over common stock (like dividends or in liquidation) and sometimes can be converted into common stock or called back by the company earlier than expected. They generally do not carry voting rights and do not have the upside growth unless they are convertible into common shares. The main differences are in the voting rights, the growth potential, and the priority in receiving dividends. If voting rights and upside growth are important, common stock would be a good choice. If income and priority in case of liquidation are important, preferred stock would be a good choice.

Bonds are a debt instrument used by governments and corporations to finance operations and projects. The investor loans money to the issuer of a bond in exchange for interest payments (based on the "coupon rate") and the eventual return of principal (at the "maturity" date). There are many different types of bonds with varying levels of complexity and a secondary market in which investors can buy and sell bonds from other investors. They have traditionally been used as a way to source income. You would buy a bond with a lump sum of money to receive periodic interest payments to cover your expenses. Years later, you would receive your initial investment back when the bond matures, or you could sell it on the secondary market prior to that point.

Mutual Funds and Bond Funds are groups of stocks or bonds made into one security. They are designed to make diversification easier for the average investor. They are usually actively managed and carry expenses for the management service. They do not trade during the day as transactions are completed at the close of the market each trading day. Index funds are the passively managed cousins of mutual and bond funds. They track an index and thus carry a lower expense because much of the work needed to run them is administrative.

Exchange-Traded Funds (ETFs) are similar to the other funds in the sense they allow you to invest in hundreds of companies in one fund, but they allow for buying and selling throughout the trading day and are taxed differently.

Derivatives are contracts that track the price of underlying assets such as stocks, bonds, and commodities or interest rates. They can be used to create income, speculate, or hedge risk for certain businesses. For example, if you expect the price of a stock to rise, you could buy an option that allows you to buy the stock at the price it is right now. This is different than actually buying the stock. If the price does rise, you are allowed to buy the stock at a "discount."

Margin accounts are loans provided by brokerages. They provide money for you to make investments, carry an interest rate, and back your cash and investments. They carry a risk that if you purchase securities that lose value, you still owe what you borrowed. The positive feature is you can make investments you would otherwise not have been able to make by borrowing money.

With advanced techniques being so readily available, it is very important that investors are aware of what they are participating in. Anyone can share their opinions, ideas, and "wins" to the world. Make sure sources are credible and look for those that provide education. You'll want to know all the rules and regulations in a market before you participate in it.

Remember the foundation of personal finance is a solid budget. If you plan for derivatives, that's fine, as long as they are not replacing items like your emergency fund. Don't forget your piggy bank!

Crosby also cleverly worded one of the main hypotheses of this book by saying, "You see yourself making life-altering financial decisions on the same device you use to check Twitter and send a goofy meme to your parents or your friends and so I think the stakes can seem low when they are in fact quite high." Technology has brought together two drastically different parts of our lives.

SUPPORTING WHAT YOU CARE ABOUT

More important than the type of investments we make is what we are actually supporting when we invest.

I've had the pleasure of being a part of some amazing charitable events in my life. I've seen all different kinds of ways to raise money for good causes. I've seen dinners, concerts, BINGO, carwashes, comedy events, recitals, dances, talent shows, speeches, conferences, and sporting events. Each of them has their own benefits, but universally there is some sort of entertainment in exchange for money that goes to cover the cost of the event and support a charity.

There are more than 1.5 million registered charities in the United States as of 2020. That's a lot of causes! I think it's great there are that many organizations dedicated to helping a specific cause. They all have to raise funds one way or another. Some have endowments that are invested and fund what they do, while others have events like the ones I have attended. Still others have fundraising campaigns more targeted toward individual donors.

With so many charities, types of events, and causes, it can be confusing as to what or where you should give your money. Big events are great ways for organizations to provide entertainment for people that will attract them and ultimately lead them to support the cause financially. Sadly, not every cause is something you'll want to celebrate. There is risk in philanthropy.

A "WALK" IN THE ZOO

One specific event I attended sticks out to me. I was asked to put a team together for a "walk." Many of the walks I have attended are a great time. It may seem like walking is a pretty boring activity, but it's something most people can do and it's easy to communicate while doing it. It's a chance to exercise a little, have some social time, and celebrate all the great things and people involved in a cause. It's more than walking and donations. It can also be a little easier on a non-profit's budget. It doesn't take a lot of money for people to walk. The cost of operating a fundraiser, once identified, would be a non-discretionary expense when put into the budgeting context.

In my experience, the best events are celebrations. A lot of organizations are supporting a complicated and troubling cause that does not lend itself to an uplifting environment. Events need to be a celebration of the great work that has been accomplished. Awards, music, and games are great. Activities are essential.

The walk I participated in was at a zoo with an event center and theme park-type attractions. It was an excellent venue. The celebration made me feel like volunteering and raising money for the cause was a great thing.

The event began with a D.J. and various food offerings. You could walk around, network, sample different foods, visit tables with information related to the cause, and even dance. Eventually, they made announcements about all the great things that had been done. They gave away all kinds of merchandise and celebrated the largest donors and the total amount the event raised. After an hour or two, it was time for the "walk."

Some walks are simply around a track. They work great, but this event was even better. You got to walk around the zoo. It wasn't a charted path either. It was like visiting the zoo for a couple of hours.

I love animals. Zoos are an excellent source of entertainment. Some animals though, shouldn't be confined. While we were on our "walk," we came across an exhibit with a white lion.

This animal was amazing to look at. It must have been three hundred pounds and looked like it could jump to the sky. Yet, it was in distress. It was in a confined space that couldn't have been bigger than fifteen feet by thirty feet. I felt terrible. The poor thing was pacing and whimpering.

I understand the lion was most likely confused by the strange crowd early in the day. It was also probably in the smaller cage for a specific reason, as there was a larger space with other lions. It could have also been ill. However, no space is big enough for a lion.

It didn't ruin the day. I just felt uncomfortable about the situation the animal was in.

IMPACT INVESTING

I wish I would have considered more closely the risk of my efforts. I interviewed Sylvia Brown on the podcast I host, *Speaking of Impact*, and she provided some excellent reasons and examples of how to evaluate the organizations you are considering supporting. She is the firstborn of the eleventh generation of the Brown family that is known for founding Brown University in Rhode Island. In her work, she develops courses and other educational materials that make "smart donors." She has also done research and speaks about the joy of giving, which is an important addition to Chapter 14.

Similar to my experience with the lion, would the things you are investing in make you feel uncomfortable about what you're supporting?

We weren't typical customers at the zoo, but we were indirectly supporting it. I am sure there was some sort of fee the charity had to pay to the zoo to use the facility for that length of time. If not, it was certainly getting plenty of publicity and attention. We had to pay for parking too.

We have the power to make a statement with how we spend our money or time as consumers. Unfortunately, it's not always easy to understand what statement we are making. You may not realize it but scrolling your Facebook feed for two hours sends a pretty strong message to the algorithm (and consequently makes the company ad revenue). I encourage you to consider all angles before giving resources to a new cause or business.

In addition to what you are buying and what charities you are supporting, you also need to know what you are investing in. The stocks and bonds (and the funds that hold them) you invest in provide support for the companies that issue them. There are other things to consider about investing than just money or returns. You may want to know what product or service a company offers, where they are located, the quality of the working conditions, the mission, or the environmental footprint. It's similar to choosing which charitable causes you support.

ESG

There is evidence it has become more popular to consider the impact of what you are investing in. The public nature of the business that corporations do allows us to be wise about what companies we support. ESG funds (environmental, social, governance) are those that apply certain principles to their investment choices to support sustainability.

The phrase "do well by doing good" has often been attributed to Benjamin Franklin. Franklin lived in the 1700s, but the modern world has brought the saying back to life. It is possible to earn money and do great things for society at the same time.

CNBC reported that ESG funds received $51 billion of new money in 2020 (up from $21 billion in 2019), accounting for about a quarter of all money that was invested in mutual funds. That's a lot of money, which shows responsible investing is becoming more popular. In 2014, only 1 percent of money was invested in ESG options. There is quite a bit of movement in this space.

ESG funds use negative screens to filter out companies that do not meet the needed criteria. There are also some funds that have positive screens that require a specific standard to be acceptable. There is no one authority that determines what makes a fund ESG. As this space becomes more popular, it's likely a more specific standard will arise.

In 2006, The United Nations rolled out its Principles for Responsible Investing (PRI). There are six principles:

1. We will incorporate ESG issues into investment analysis and decision-making processes.
2. We will be active owners and incorporate ESG issues into our ownership policies and practices.

3. We will seek appropriate disclosure on ESG issues by the entities in which we invest.
4. We will promote acceptance and implementation of the Principles within the investment industry.
5. We will work together to enhance our effectiveness in implementing the Principles.
6. We will each report on our activities and progress toward implementing the Principles.

They have an academy that allows people and organizations to train in ESG. It will become important to meet the PRI standards moving forward, especially as investors seek an authority that recognizes who is participating in PRI.

There are other terms you should be aware of in addition to ESG.

Socially responsible investing (SRI) is a form of investing that focuses specifically on the social impact of the investments you make. It concentrates on things like sustainable initiatives for Earth, human rights, and consumer protection.

Biblically responsible investing (BRI) is a form of investing that focuses on using Biblical principles in the investment process. This form of investing draws on scripture and applies things like seeking wise counsel, eliminating debt, avoiding speculation, diversification, avoiding procrastination, planning for the future, considering the needs of others, stewardship, and the belief humans are not investing for themselves but for God.

Regardless of which title you give to your approach, it is important to consider the things that mean the most to you. If you know what is most important, you can apply those values to your choices.

It will be hard to have one overarching rule set we can all apply to impact investing because we all have different needs and values. As resources grow, you can go to multiple sources to gather information, but you'll need to select what metrics and measurement points mean the most to you.

The nature of ESG lends itself to sound decision-making. You have to consider the investments you are making in a deeper fashion than you would if you were speculating about a hot buy you caught on the internet. You should consider all the points of any investment regardless of what it is or how it's categorized.

INVEST WISELY IN YOURSELF AND OTHERS

The investment you make in a company, organization, or event supports something directly and likely other things indirectly. I was happy to directly support the charity that held the walk at the zoo. It was the indirect support of the caged lion that made me uncomfortable. I now consider the treatment of animals a risk in my charitable and financial growth efforts. I will always keep that in the back of my mind when investing in causes and companies for the rest of my life.

Once you've established your budget, built your emergency fund, and paid off your debt, you're ready to invest. It can be an exciting step in your financial life. Use your curiosity as a source of motivation for research and informed decisions, not speculating and chasing the latest stock tip to hit the impatient newswire that is digital media. In addition, make yourself aware of what your money is going to support. It's better to know in advance than to find out after some time that you've been contributing to something that makes you uncomfortable. This is a risk not worth taking.

8.

All That Glitters Is Not Gold, Including Cryptocurrency

———

THE MONEY OF THE FUTURE IS HERE

What if your piggy bank was digital? The way you handled your "loose change" would be a lot different.

The first time I ever experienced a digital money system other than that which is based on the US dollar was when I went to college. My undergraduate school, Hofstra University, had meal plans. Your student identification card carried a limited number of points per semester. It was hardly an adequate amount for a college athlete.

The digital point system made acquiring a meal rather easy, too easy to be honest. It was convenient, but rationing was imperative. You could easily overspend your points early in a semester and starve at the back end. It was a much different system than I was used to when back at home. It took some time to adjust as I was forced to participate.

Today, there is a new digital money system that will require quite an adjustment for most of us.

DIFFERENT MONEY SYSTEMS

As the world changes, we are constantly adapting to new things. We study differently. We are entertained differently. We communicate in more modern ways. We also hold our money in a different way than our ancestors did. In the modern world, we are not only changing the way we store our money, but we are also changing the way we think about it. We are even exploring a completely different monetary system that would not only change the type of currency we use but also how we should consider storing and investing it. Understanding the ideology of a system is imperative to making wise decisions within it.

At my employer that I mentioned in Chapter 5, we went through compensation changes multiple times in the twelve years I was involved. Every time they changed the system, everyone in my position (one of variable pay) had to look at their business and recalculate all their projections. Operating as if the old system existed could lead to critical failure. Thankfully, we were usually given an advance notice of months to prepare. Imagine if there was a new type of money or the whole world changed its monetary system?

Cryptocurrency is here. It will be important to understand what it is and how it works moving forward. As of April 2021, there were more than ten thousand cryptocurrencies. None of them are guaranteed to survive. In fact, over one thousand have come and gone.

Different forms of currency are nothing new to our world. There have been numerous types since early times. These days, digitization is very prominent. Forms like Bitcoin and Ethereum are investments for many people and can be grouped alongside asset classes such as large and small-sized stocks. However, what sets cryptocurrency apart is its decentralization. It's a different system than that of the fiat system most of us are used to.

The United States dollar is backed by the government and is a legal form of payment as part of the fiat system currently in place. Its supply is controlled (at least in part) by a central bank. Cryptocurrency does not have a central bank. It is controlled by those who hold it. With that being said, the same principles of understanding for the other types of investments should be applied here as well. The basis of understanding cryptocurrency, however, is more about a philosophy, a monetary system, and economics.

Decentralization is the scenario where there is no one authority. In the case of money, there is no central bank. There is an agreed-upon protocol that must be followed to participate. In the world of cryptocurrency, there must be a reliable, impossibly challenging to cheat, and consistent way of tracking transactions. This is done through extremely powerful computing that requires energy to execute. There is an electronic ledger that can be reviewed at any time. All transactions ever made are traceable.

MINING A LIMITED SUPPLY

The people who verify Bitcoin blockchain transactions are called miners. They are rewarded in Bitcoin (or the other appropriate currency) for confirming these transactions. Seems simple enough, right? Actually, it's an arduous process. Transactions are grouped into one-megabyte (1MB) blocks. Detailed information technology is certainly beyond the scope of this text, but a basic understanding of electronic storage is needed to follow the process. Miners are in a "race" to verify transactions. Not only do they have to compute 1MB of information, but they have to be the first one to do so (accurately) to be rewarded. Needless to say, professional mining is not a career path for many.

Specific to Bitcoin, there will only be twenty-one million ever made. This creates an increase in value over time that is counter to the current money system which can create "new dollars" and cause inflation. This is covered in the next chapter. Interestingly, there is likely to be less than twenty-one million ever in circulation because of people who may lose their tokens or die with them. There is no way to (legally) create more bitcoins.

The most prominent explanation for the exact twenty-one million limit is related to the world's money supply ($21 trillion) at the time of Bitcoin's creation. If bitcoin were to replace all the currencies in that figure, each would be worth $1 million, and each Satoshi (1 one hundred-millionth of a bitcoin) would be worth $.01.

SATOSHI NAKAMOTO

Satoshis are named after Bitcoin's creator, Satoshi Nakamoto. This is generally considered pseudonymous. The person or people have never been identified. All that is known is Nakamoto authored the Bitcoin whitepaper in 2008, began developing blockchain software in 2009, supported decentralized finance (the ability for investors to deal directly with each other instead of a centralized authority), and sent a final e-mail (the only method of communication they used) in 2010. It's rather mysterious, but the detailed calculations, the overall brain power invested, and the specificity of the system cannot be overlooked.

MULTIPLE FORMS OF CRYPTO

There are many other cryptocurrencies, as mentioned above, and many of them are inspired by Nakamoto and Bitcoin. Ethereum is considered to be the next most prominent form, and while it also uses blockchain technology, it has many other nuances. It is being used for other complex processes such as payments, lending, underwriting, and portfolio management. Each form of cryptocurrency is unique, and I must stress the need to understand before investing.

Bitcoin was the first of its kind and it seems to have quite a head start on its competitors. Lyn Alden, the founder of Lyn Alden Investment Strategy, provides an interesting analogy highly relevant to this text. She compares cryptocurrency to a social network. Alden's electronics engineering training and investment studies provide a unique perspective on the subject. Starting another community like Facebook would be impossible not because of the technical coding needed to create the software, but because of the volume of users needed to compete. Alden writes, "The more people that use one, the more people it attracts, in a self-reinforcing virtuous network effect, and this makes it more and more valuable over time." This also applies to cryptocurrencies. Bitcoin has had more time to develop its network than its competitors.

Storing cryptocurrencies is also something that needs to be understood. When dealing with this type of technology, security is extremely important. Coins and tokens can be stolen. It's not easy to steal them, but a challenge never stopped criminals before. You can't put Bitcoin in a safety deposit box, and to spend it, it must be accessed through the internet. For example, to transact business, you would need to have a "warm" connection or "warm wallet." It's warm because it's accessible (or susceptible) through the internet. You probably don't want all your cryptocurrency available at any given time. For safe storage, you might use a "cold wallet." This is digital storage that is not connected to the internet. In theory, it is un-hackable.

There are many places to assist with the purchase and storage of cryptocurrencies. Although not the reason why you should make a decision as to which currency to buy or which company to do business with, Coin Market Cap provides data on the market capitalization of the different coins and the trading volume on the different exchanges. Market capitalization is the total value of all the coins of a given type that have been mined, and volume is the total amount of coins traded in a given period.

A GOLD REPLACEMENT?

Some people believe cryptocurrencies will replace gold someday. Alex Gladstein, chief strategy officer of the Human Rights Foundation, believes Bitcoin is well on its way. As of early 2021, total gold was valued at about $8 trillion, and Bitcoin was $1 trillion. It has been around twelve years, and over the next twelve it will reduce gold to having only industrial and cosmetic value. It's currently worth 1/8 of all the gold in the world. Yet, despite the current value difference, they have some things in common. First of all, neither can be destroyed. They are each durable. They are also considered to be fungible, or pieces are mutually interchangeable. Each bitcoin or equal amount of bullion is worth the same. Each is divisible. Gold can be smelted, and bitcoins (other cryptocurrencies have different smaller increments) have Satoshis (0.00000001 Bitcoin).

At the beginning of the second quarter of 2021, one Bitcoin was worth north of $55,000. Satoshis provide a smaller increment, enabling smaller transactions and amounts of ownership. Gold and cryptocurrencies are also portable. They can be transferred. A cryptocurrency supporter would argue digital forms are better because transporting them is much easier. Could you imagine having to ship gold to buy something?

Gladstein says the cryptocurrency is a valuable form of money and the application of Gresham's law points to how the newer technology is affecting the way people think about money. The law, although not foolproof, states "bad money drives out good." It was coined in 1558 by the economist H.D. Macleod after Sir Thomas Gresham. Gresham was not the first to study the concept, but he was able to clarify how people were prone to holding what was considered to have more value while spending what was thought to be of lesser value. This infers that Bitcoin is of more value. People are spending dollars and other forms of currency with the intent of holding their Bitcoin. The "bad money" is being circulated while the "good money" is being held as a store of value.

Gladstein believes Bitcoin holders, or Hodlers (slang for someone who is holding), have a different philosophy of money. He said, "Because of the nature of the asset and the way that it's monetizing and growing in value and the way that it promises, due to its structure and absolute scarcity, to be more valuable in twenty years than today. It's changing the mindset of people who use it, and people are becoming more thrifty, efficient, and more interested in saving." He added, "All of a sudden, thinking low-time preference and saving for the future is sexy." This is fascinating because digital technology is generally associated with high-time preference and higher transaction volume. In addition, we are using a centuries-old concept of currency and applying it to the most modern form we have. Chapter 12 will spend more time on long-term savings, but this is a solid practice and is more prudent than speculative investing.

A FREEDOM TOOL
At a certain point, and already for some, cryptocurrencies could be more valuable than their native currency. Gladstein also mentioned, "People can use it as a shield to defend themselves" in response to an authoritarian government. They can own currency without anyone else knowing how much,

and its value can't be inflated or deflated by another party. In this case, we may be closer to the rapid circulation of Bitcoin than many think.

As early as 2015, there was the development of what is called the Lighting Network. This is a payment system that acts on top of the Bitcoin protocol, allowing for easier transactions. It will make smaller payments more appealing, faster, and safer. There are limitations, but it's evolving.

Bitcoin and its fellow digital assets do shine in some of the same ways that gold and other commodities do, but they are a much different asset overall. They "glitter," but aren't gold.

Despite the complexity of Bitcoin, many people invested in the asset in 2020. According to UpMyInterest, its most recent annual returns are as follows:

2017—1318 percent
2018—-72.6 percent
2019—87.2 percent
2020—302.8 percent

This is quite a wide array of returns. The volatility must be considered. It is possible Bitcoin replaces the United States dollar as the world reserve currency. This would require a switch from the current fiat system we employ to the decentralized system many cryptocurrencies promote. If this is the case, the current volatility would be worth experiencing, but this is very uncertain. If it does act like its relative gold, then it could be a nice hedge to the traditional markets. Gladstein noted cryptocurrencies can be transferred faster than gold, and their rise has happened much more quickly than that of their precious metal counterpart. We are still at the point of predictions, and depending on what media you experience, you will get differing opinions on what to do.

LEGAL TENDER

During my research for this book, El Salvador announced Bitcoin would become legal tender in the country on September 7, 2021. It did not replace the US dollar but joined it. It is the first country to commit to cryptocurrency as a part of its system. In fact, every adult that downloads and registers the government's crypto application will receive $30 worth of Bitcoin. It's important to note the government does not control this money like other governments control the monies of their countries. It has simply made businesses accept it as a form of payment. One country of this size does not indicate a change in the global system, but it's a big step for digital money. It remains an investment of increasing popularity for the rest of us at this time.

I suggest acquiring as much information as you can before making any investment with added stress in the crypto space.

It would be foolish to solely consult a source strongly in favor of any specific side or concept because the story and motives across the different forms are just too inconsistent. For example, Bitcoin started as a new currency system proposed in a newsletter by Satoshi Nakamoto. Dogecoin, which was actually started as a joke, received much fanfare in April 2020 when it started a meteoric rise from $0.06–$0.70 in a month's time. With the advent of immediate reporting, "smart ads," and "retargeting," these large price shifts can generate lots of publicity and it can be very easy to travel deeply into the rabbit hole of a single ideology or coin.

Gather information as you like, pull yourself out of the hole if needed, and check into other sources. This is not the type of investment to let your impatient, "on-demand" mind lead your purchase. If you are watching recorded television, don't skip the commercials! Take your time on this one.

We are currently in the advance notice stage as I was in my previous career. We have been alerted of a new system, and you should familiarize yourself with it while you can. There is the possibility of it losing traction and crashing completely, leaving bitcoiners and owners of other crypto with no value. If it ends up becoming the world's system of choice or somewhere in between, you'll be in a much better position to manage your finances at that point.

9.

He Who Pays the Piper Calls the Tune

———

WHO RUNS OUR ECONOMIC SYSTEM?

The greatest leaders have the best interest of the people they lead in mind. They do their job by promoting the success of others.

Have you ever been part of a group, team, or company that lacked great leadership? There's no chance of success if you don't know what the goal is or if the people in charge aren't focused on helping everyone execute their responsibilities. You don't want to be working against the leaders.

The existing economic system has a certain way of leading us and is designed to seek stability. It is important to understand how and why things are done and how to make decisions with those in mind. Otherwise, you'll be working against the forces in charge. Education is a must.

THE CLASSROOM EXPERIENCE

It's exciting and necessary to look to the future as we did in the previous chapter. However, the current system is most relevant, and any decisions we make now are within it. Financial management is a process that requires an understanding of the system you live in, the authorities that run it, and the ability to operate with the rules set forth. It's similar to a classroom where we are the students. We hope the teacher is acting in our best interest.

The mark of a good teacher is someone who creates a desire to learn in the students. They are a selfless leader.

A student who wants to learn is one who will. Desire is a powerful force. I am certain you will learn about our economic system in this chapter because you are making the effort to read.

I can attribute much of my learning to great educators who made learning enjoyable. The most indelible lessons are those I sought. I can't criticize curriculums and standardized testing because assessing progress is absolutely necessary. However, if the sole reason for learning is just for the marks, the lessons do not last. Thankfully, there is no quiz at the end of this text.

I believe if a good teacher is one who makes learning desired, it is the students' classroom experience that indicates the quality of the instructor.

I've had the pleasure of being married to a kindergarten teacher for much of my adult life. The lessons you can learn from five- and six-year-old people are amazing. Watching how they act and listening to their words can provide much wisdom.

It usually goes unnoticed, but there is a lot of preparation that goes into a classroom every year before the students even arrive. A teacher has to make visuals to put on the walls, lesson plans, and set up a seating arrangement. They have to think about the ways that will be best for the students to learn the subject matter, interact with each other, and find joy throughout the day. It is not uncommon for a teacher to spend two weeks setting up the classroom prior to the beginning of the school year.

Despite all the preparation for a year, a teacher never knows exactly what is in store for an upcoming class. Every group is unique. There are different amounts of students, different personalities, and different levels of intelligence. In any scenario, though, it is the teacher's job to create an environment where learning is desired. If learning is desired, everything else will fall into place.

The uniqueness of each class means all the preparation in the world and the perfect vision for a class cannot guarantee there will be success. A teacher will begin noticing the unique aspects of a new class immediately and must adapt by adjusting throughout the year.

Of all the years of my wife's employment, one sticks out the most. In 2013, she had a class that was wild and tough to manage. They didn't seem to follow directions as well as others. It felt like she and her assistant were constantly telling the students "no," and by the time the holiday season came, they were worn down.

Throughout that first semester of the year, they used various techniques to try to fix the environment. They threatened to eliminate recess or other fun activities. They implemented silent time. They even had some parent-teacher conferences to try to help the students calm down. Nothing seemed to be effective, and their patience was thin after a tough few months.

In early January, about halfway through the school year, my wife and her assistant went to a short teacher's conference that was about student behavior. It was just what the education doctor ordered. They learned various things that could be useful, but one was a classroom changer.

Praising students for their good behavior was more important than focusing on bad behavior.

Upon returning to the classroom, my wife and her assistant decided to implement their new technique. They focused more on praising the good things. For example, if student "A" and student "B" were sitting together and student "A" was being disruptive while student "B" was sitting quietly, they would praise student "B" for good behavior rather than critiquing student "A." This created a desire in student "A" to be praised themselves. In turn, misbehaving students began to act appropriately because it was shown that this type of behavior came with positive feedback. Amazingly, there was an immediate change in the classroom when they implemented this strategy.

This classroom experience shows there is no perfect solution for a teacher to "fix" his or her class. A school year is a long journey, and it takes time and multiple adjustments for a teacher to accomplish the main goal (making learning desirable). My wife's students from the 2013 school year suddenly enjoyed learning when praises were a focus. Other classes needed different adjustments. One thing, however, is constant: it is up to the teacher to make the adjustments so the class as a whole has the best experience it can.

THE CURRENT ECONOMIC SYSTEM

Just as a classroom is an ever-morphing environment, so is an economy. It is important that as our world and economics change, the next generations are taught how our systems work so they can make informed decisions. The best economies are those without disruption whereas many of the "students" as possible are contributing to a positive experience. A cyclical nature exists, and recession will eventually occur. However, any stage of an economic cycle is made better by cooperation and understanding of the existing situation.

The current economic system is capitalistic, and the US dollar is the world reserve currency. Bitcoin, as discussed in Chapter 8, may be challenging the current prominent monetary system, but what we have now is what we must follow.

In a capitalistic society, company ownership is by the people and not the state. In theory, this provides the opportunity for anyone to create the business of their dreams and change their way of life. This is important to note because there has to be regulation. Although the government does not own all the business (as it does in a system such as communism), it does have some authority.

THE FED

In our monetary system, there is an amount of control given to the Federal Reserve (The United States' central bank). It acts similar to a teacher as it adjusts the system giving incentives to different things.

The government directs the central bank. "The Fed" has a dual mandate from Congress. The two objectives are:

1. Price Stability
2. Maximum Sustainable Employment

These objectives indicate the Fed needs to manage inflation and the employment rate. Inflation is the concept of rising prices that make the value of currency lower. If the price of a gallon of milk inflates from $3.50 to $4.00 it means your $3.50 that you previously used to buy milk with is not worth as much as it used to be. In our system, inflation can be controlled (at least in part) by The Fed's monetary policies. In addition, monetary policies are used to affect employment rates.

The Fed is made up of three parts that contribute to its operations: the reserve banks, the Board of Governors, and the Federal Open Market Committee (FOMC). The FOMC is a twelve-member group made up of the Board of Governors, the President of the Federal Reserve Bank of New York, and a rotating set of four of the remaining eleven reserve bank presidents.

The Fed sets a target federal funds rate eight times a year. This is the rate at which banks (not the central bank) can loan each other overnight to meet reserve requirements. They are required to have certain amounts of money on deposit at the Fed to cover their obligations. To reach the target federal funds rate, the Fed will use four different tools:

1. The Discount Rate—The discount rate is the interest rate charged to commercial banks and other depository institutions on loans they receive from their regional Federal Reserve Bank. It affects the money supply, as the lower the rate, the more banks will be willing to borrow and lend out. The higher the rate, the less money that will be lent out. It is determined by the Board of Governors.
2. Reserve Requirements—Reserve requirements are the portions of deposits that banks must hold in cash, either in their vaults or on deposit at a Reserve Bank. The lower the requirement, the more money available in the banking system. This signals expansionary efforts. Higher requirements are more restrictive. The amount is also determined by the Board of Directors.
3. Open Market Operations—The purchase and sale of securities in the open market by a central bank (usually treasury bonds). These are the responsibility of the FOMC. They will either buy or sell treasury bonds. To support expansion, they will buy the bonds and push money into the system, which pushes interest rates lower as banks compete for customers and makes borrowing money more attractive. In a contractionary effort, they

will sell the bonds, pulling money out of the system and raising interest as banks attract customers and savings becomes more attractive.

4. Interest on Reserves—This is the most recent tool given to the Fed by Congress (Emergency Economic Stabilization Act of 2008). Banks are required to have reserves at the Fed as mentioned previously. Originally, the central bank could offer an interest rate on those reserves that are required (interest rate on required reserves or IORR) and those that are excess (interest rate on excess reserves or IOER). As of July 29, 2021, the IORR and IOER were each replaced with the interest rate on reserve balances (IORB). The lower the rate, the more incentive banks have to lend money out of their excess and vice versa. The Board determines this, too.

The Fed Funds Rate generally dictates where a bank's prime interest rate will land. Banks can set their "prime" rate (the rate they offer to people who carry the least amount of risk) on their own, but most will hover around three percentage points above the Fed rate.

When the FOMC wants to stimulate economic activity, they lower rates to make it easier to borrow money. This pushes more money into the system. If they wish to slow things down, they will raise interest rates. As of 2021, we have been in a low-interest-rate environment for quite some time.

CONTROLLING INTEREST RATES

The Fed has pulled the necessary levers to keep rates low since the Great Recession, which ended in 2009. This chart (of the Fed funds rate at the beginning of each year) shows how things dropped sharply during the Great Recession, began to rise slowly in 2015, and plummeted to virtually zero again due to the coronavirus pandemic in 2020. The purpose of this action was to stimulate economic activity.

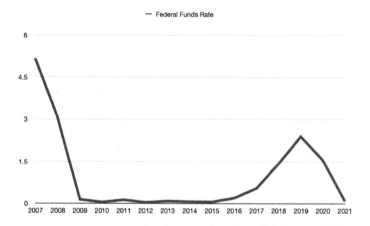

— Federal Funds Rate

Lower interest rates lead to more attractive loans for people and businesses to make purchases. It also tends to leave people with more money to spend, which encourages consumption and production by businesses. As businesses produce and sell, their stock prices are driven higher.

As you can see, there are many ways a central bank controls the system. Understanding the motive of the Fed is just as important as the actions and understanding how these relate to your personal situation is even more important. In other words, if the news comes out that the Fed is lowering interest rates, that doesn't necessarily mean you should go get a loan. It's certain banks will advertise lower rates and local realtors might indicate it's a "buyer's market." While interest rates are an important part of a mortgage, there are far more important things that should be part of your decision to buy a home. Think about the amount of money you have to put down, the amount of cash flow you have (back to the budget and piggy bank), the place you want to live, your family situation moving forward, property taxes, insurance, and resale value.

The numbers on a home loan could look good, but what if the rate decrease was the result of an unexpected recession that would severely limit your income for the near-term future? Or, what if the property values where you currently live stand to increase? You may not want to sell your house right away or leave the area. Observe what the Fed is trying to do to make financial decisions accordingly. Make the current policies work for you.

TIMING IS EVERYTHING (LUCKY FOR US)

The Great Recession, first mentioned in the Introduction, was a good example of an extreme effort by The Fed. They had to execute unprecedented actions to stabilize the system. At that time, my wife and I were just married, and she was beginning her career as a teacher (second grade at this point, a much different experience than kindergarten). What better time to buy a house?

I wish I could say I was well educated on the subject, but we seemed to luck out in buying a townhome at that point. The Fed had lowered interest rates and the real estate collapse led to some cheap properties in our town. It was definitely a buyer's market, and we would not have been able to acquire a home had the economic situation been different. We learned quickly how important it was to take advantage of the initiatives in place.

The Federal Reserve controls the money, so it gets to decide what is the economy's focus and direction. It controls money by using various techniques, and those techniques provide incentives for certain actions (like buying a house). The chairman during the Great Recession was Ben Bernanke. I believe my wife and I owe some thanks to him and his team for implementing strategies that allowed us to purchase our first home. His position is often highlighted during times of economic stress.

THE CHAIRMAN AND THE TEACHER

Jerome Powell is the sixteenth and current chairman of the Federal Reserve. In April of 2021, during the COVID-19 pandemic, he made an appearance on *60 Minutes*, CBS's famous newsmagazine show. On the show, he was clear that the Fed is not perfect and not capable of predicting all economic shifts. He said they "focus on having a strong financial system that's resilient to significant shocks." The pandemic was an enormous shock to the system as over twenty-two million Americans lost their jobs. There was no way to predict such an issue, and those are the types of shocks for which Powell and his colleagues need to prepare.

When things do happen, the Fed has to be nimble and "pull the proper levers" to navigate the uncertain. Even then, they can never be sure. Powell admitted in the interview their projected worst-case scenario was a complete catastrophe.

The Fed's actions are designed to manage the economic system, which is similar to managing a classroom. A teacher that praises good behavior provides an incentive to act well. In addition, they must prepare students in case of emergency. In Florida, my wife has to prepare her classroom in case hurricane-force winds threaten the school building. In other areas, the threat could be flash flooding or earthquakes. Unfortunately, every school has active shooter training now. You never know exactly when something tragic could happen.

A good teacher and a good "Fed" make the environment they are in charge of run smoothly during normal times, and during emergencies they rely on the tools they have and their preparations to lessen the effects of the issue. They are invested in the process, and it behooves them to foster an environment of growth (academic or financial). Therefore, they call the tune.

From a psychological perspective, understanding the economic system will help you avoid potentially disappointing efforts as you make decisions that affect your long-term financial situation. You may not agree with all the policies in place and the tools used by the Fed or your teacher, but it can be frustrating to operate against the grain. Understand the system in place and use it to your advantage.

CREDIBLE INFORMATION

The role technology plays in our economic system is key. The spread of information is rapid, and the advertising policies referenced in section one of this book are at work. The good news is just about anyone can get any information they want. The bad news is just about anyone can share information whether accurate or not. Also, anyone can advertise what they want with limited restrictions.

Make sure you understand what information you need and seek answers from trusted sources. No organization is required to review economic policy prior to selling its products or services. A business will gladly spike its prices if people are willing and able to pay. It's the Fed's job to keep prices stable, but it's ultimately up to us consumers to make wise purchasing decisions.

I wouldn't say you should review economics prior to going out to eat or buying a new pair of shoes. However, big purchases that may require borrowing money like a home or car are greatly affected by the current situation. Use technology in these scenarios to review current loan rates, rate projections, and market conditions.

The sale your local car dealer advertised on Instagram is not necessarily a reason to buy a new car, and it certainly doesn't take into account what current economic policy means for consumers. You may find a little patience could save you some money when you purchase and a lot of money down the road.

Now that we've examined the macroeconomic system we live in, we can apply it to personal finance. The next chapter covers how the policies above affect the borrowing and lending of money and ultimately how it's paid back.

10.

You Feel Like a Million Bucks

———

BORROWING MONEY AND YOUR CREDIT

Have you ever felt the stress of an exam you have to pass for an education credit, professional designation, or a license? It's a nerve-racking feeling. The worst part is when you have to click "submit" at the very end. The moment while the page loads before flashing a red or green screen is terrible. If it's green, it's just a relief. If it's red, you feel like a failure and you don't receive your certificate.

The great thing about the monetary system we employ is that it is flexible. We can make mistakes and still be okay. It's possible to be short on your budget and make up the difference. At the same time, it's also possible to pay more than you might have for something if you believe it to be a valuable transaction. You should be careful not to abuse this privilege, but it's great to have it. In fact, it's essential in our system because lending money is a big part of what makes it run. It's up to you to borrow (and lend) wisely.

ACCESS TO MONEY

On Wednesday, March 10th, 2021, Dallas Cowboys owner Jerry Jones said, "Most anything I have ever been involved in, that ends up being special, I overpaid for. Every time. To the end. Anytime I've tried to get a bargain, I got just that. It was a bargain (laughs) in a lot of ways, and not up to standard."

Debt and lending are a big part of macro-finance. In turn, they are also a big part of personal finance. Like Jerry, it may make sense for you to overpay for something. If you need to borrow to make it happen, do it wisely.

The access to money can make you feel like a million bucks, or at least that you have a million bucks when you really don't. Our system is such that you can't do a lot of things without having some sort of loan. Buying a home is the most prominent example, but many people buy their car with a loan, and as you know, others often get payday loans to pay their bills. Understanding what you are paying for is essential.

Let's look at an example of a six-year auto loan for a car with a purchase price of $30,000 and a sales tax of 1.25 percent. You made a $5,000 down payment and the Annual Percentage Rate (APR) of interest is 4 percent. Here's how it breaks down:

Amount You Borrowed—$25,000
Your Monthly Payment—$391.13
Your Total in 72 monthly payments—$28,161.33
Your Total Interest Paid—$3,161.33
Sales Tax—$375
The Total Transaction—$33,536.33

It may feel good to get a new $30,000 car, but you should consider how much it actually costs you. This example illustrates interest costs of more than 10.5 percent of the purchase price and more than 12.5 percent of the amount you borrowed while taxes were just 1.5 percent and 1.25 percent, respectively. The access to the money cost you well more than the tax on the purchase.

MORTGAGES

Lending institutions know most people need a loan to buy a home. There isn't a whole lot of room for negotiation because most are seeking their dream and need a home to live in. You see your friend's brand-new house in a completely different part of the country (or world), and you think you deserve the same. If you've been home shopping before, you might have felt the feeling of "this is it!" You feel that when one home sticks out more than the others and you're willing to do whatever it takes to make a deal happen.

The first home my wife and I bought (the one from Chapter 9) gave us the most amazing feeling. Looking back, it may have been a little inflated, but it was our first big purchase together. I am not sure if there was anything that could have stopped us outside of not being approved for our mortgage. It turned out to be a good move as the price of the townhome was lower than the local market, and home prices rose for the four years we lived there.

I wish I could say I researched and expected the scenario to play out as it did. However, it was more luck than anything. We barely qualified for the loan, and the home needed a lot of work. Thankfully, our families were so excited for us that they helped improve it in many ways. If home values went down, we didn't fix it up, one of us lost our jobs, or I mismanaged my variable income outlined in Chapter 5, we would have been in trouble. I realized how much we benefited from that place when we sold it.

Chase your dreams but be wise. Make your decision with the long-term viability of a potential thirty-year relationship with the lender in mind and the dwelling you will make your home in. Don't solely rely on the beautiful pictures the realtor sent you.

Consider the term (usually between ten to thirty years) of the loan, the initial interest rate, if and how the rate can change (they can be fixed or variable, be careful), how much money you have to put down, primary mortgage insurance (a lender's usual requirement for loans with less than 20 percent of the purchase price put down at closing, PMI), your property taxes, homeowner's association (HOA) dues, a realtor's commission, the cost of utilities in that area, the quality of local schools, other local things of note, and other expenses. Each of these will carry a different weight for your situation. You may be your own realtor, or not have children. Also, you should consider how much, if any, of your mortgage payment is tax-deductible. This is a benefit, but not a reason to buy a home or spend more.

It's also important to consider your emotions when shopping for a home. In a seller's market (as is the case as I write this book), there is a strong possibility you are not the only person who wants the home at which you are looking. Dale

Vermillion is a renowned mortgage consultant and author of *Navigating the Mortgage Maze*. In an appearance on the *MoneyWise* radio show, he said, "We get emotionally caught up. Especially when we start talking about negotiating and bidding on a home. Number one, make sure you are absolutely prepared before you ever go into a purchase transaction and you've already established what is my maximum I'm going to pay... You cannot go in and just start to bid and get caught up in the frenzy of the bidding war." The items above should help you come up with that maximum amount. Ultimately, the purchase price is the number that has the largest effect on your personal financial situation.

Other loans that apply to your home are refinances (which are similar to original mortgages) and home equity lines of credit (HELOQ). In all cases, make sure you understand the terms before you "mentally" make a big purchase.

STUDENT LOANS

Another big part of our system is student loans. Investopedia lists three eye-popping statistics as of September 9, 2021:

1. $1.57 trillion in outstanding student loan debt
2. 54 percent of college attendees are taking on debt
3. $34,455 average amount of student loan debt per borrower

Some would call this the epidemic that preceded COVID-19. Student loans are very nuanced. They carry some nice features compared to other loans but also have drawbacks. Funding advanced education also comes with certain tax benefits and credits. These, like home loans, should be considered along with all of the other features before applying for a loan.

A college education is usually expected these days. I am a firm believer that a four-year university education is not the proper road for everyone. It could be easy to "fall in line" with the rest of your high school classmates and attend a desirable state university. Education is something that should last a lifetime. The four years (more or less) after college should not be the only contributor to your advanced learning. For some people, it doesn't make sense to spend tens of thousands of dollars (or more) to do what everyone else is doing.

Careers in law, finance, or medicine often require an education that could lead to excessive student debt. Yet, they may also provide a salary capable of paying off that debt in a reasonable amount of time. In contrast, patrol officers, bus/truck drivers, medical technicians, firefighters, and plumbers usually do not require a degree. These and many others would not come with steep education debt.

If you or your children do decide traditional college is appropriate, it's important to make wise funding decisions. Some people are fortunate enough to receive a partial or full scholarship. These can be athletic, academic, or based on other factors. I encourage people to pursue these heavily in the areas they excel.

Outside of scholarships, there is also government assistance for some people. Most importantly, you will need to fill out the Free Application for Federal Student Aid (FAFSA form).

Nerd Wallet has an excellent guide for working through the process.

There are many sources for assistance with paying for college. In some cases, you can negotiate the cost of tuition. It's a good idea to provide the stated expense for other schools to which you have been accepted. Also, you can apply for a work-study (which is tied to your FAFSA status) or a teaching assistant (TA) position. Of course, you can also work and go to school at the same time.

If a loan is an appropriate course, you'll have four main options. The first three offer different forms of forbearance, deferment, and favorable repayment options:

1. Subsidized—your interest is covered while you are in school and you don't have to start paying anything back for a period after you graduate (currently six months).
2. Unsubsidized—the interest accrues from the beginning, and you don't have to start paying anything back for a period after you graduate (currently six months).
3. Parent PLUS—the loan is the responsibility of the parent(s) of the student, interest accrues from the start, and the deferment until six months after graduation may apply.
4. Private—generally carry higher interest rates and do not come with some of the features that the above options do.

Erin Lowry also covers this subject in *Broke Millennial*. She says, "The government is a far more benevolent lender than private entities." The first three options are generally more attractive than private options. It is good to know they are an option. Start with the government assistance first.

CREDIT CARDS

While a home mortgage, a car loan, and student loans are a must for many, other debts are not. Credit cards have a lot of great features. They are convenient. They provide fraud protection. They can cover you in a bind. Some provide legitimate discounts and benefits. However, the interest rates are very high. According to WalletHub, the average rate is above 17 percent. This is far from mortgages, which can be below 3 percent here in 2021.

Buying now and paying later feels like a great luxury but paying more later is not actually a luxury. It would make more sense to avoid making a discretionary purchase and save up to buy the item with cash when you have enough money.

Some places offer no-interest financing to entice you to still buy. If you use one of these options, you have to make sure you pay off the loan before the no-interest period is over. The lender is not likely to push you to pay it off before then.

Divide the number of months of no-interest financing that you have into the amount borrowed (usually you have to pay some upfront) and add an "envelope" in your budget for that amount. It has become a non-discretionary expense. Many of these arrangements require you to pay a certain amount per month anyway. Making it part of your budget will ensure you don't get surprised with a huge sum to pay the last month of the no-interest period or a bill with interest on it.

PAYDAY LOANS

Payday loans are a very different type of loan and even more expensive than the others. They take what might seem like a smaller percentage but are applied over a much shorter period of time.

A two-week payday loan usually costs $15 per $100. If you borrowed $100 for a two-week payday loan at that rate, it would seem like a simple 15 percent interest ($15). Since you have to repay the loan in two weeks, your annual rate would be an APR of nearly 400 percent, making you pay almost four times the amount you borrowed. At $15 over two weeks (fourteen days), that equals $1.07 per day. The total of $1.07 multiplied by 365 days is $390.55. Some payday loans can have an effective rate as high as 1,900 percent.

If you don't pay one of these types of loans back promptly, you could easily find interest rate percentages in the hundreds or higher when extrapolated out over months or a year. Proceed with caution. These should be avoided if possible and definitely not used for discretionary purchases.

CREDIT

There are many types of loans, and most of them require an examination of your credit or your ability to acquire goods and services based on the trust that you will make future payments.

Lending money carries a risk. Lenders will put their borrowers through an underwriting process. This is to assess the risk of lending you money. The most important part of this evaluation is your credit score which measures your credit-worthiness—your ability to pay back a loan. There are multiple ways to measure your credit, but the most prominent is a FICO score. It is used in 90 percent of credit applications.

The FICO score was developed by Fair, Isaac, and Company, a data analytics organization most widely known for its credit score. Scores can range from 300 to 850, with the higher numbers being better. There are three credit bureaus that report scores. They each use slightly different versions of FICO and each should be consulted to ensure the accuracy of your situation.

In 2003, the Fair and Accurate Credit Transactions Act (FACTA) states that consumers are entitled to one free report from each bureau every year. The three organizations are Equifax, TransUnion, and Experian. These are not to be confused with Standard & Poor's, Fitch, and Moody's, which provide credit ratings for corporations and not individuals.

There are five factors, with different weights, that determine your credit score:

- **Payment history (35 percent):** This measures the timeliness of your payments.
- **Amounts owed (30 percent):** This measures the amount of debt you have relative to your credit limits.
- **Length of credit history (15 percent):** This measures the amount of time you've had credit.
- **New credit (10 percent):** This measures the frequency at which you attempt to acquire credit.

- **Credit mix (10 percent):** This measures the diversity of your types of credit.

In 2006, Equifax, TransUnion, and Experian created a new credit score called the VantageScore. It is designed to be more appropriate for modern data collections and behavioral trends. Technology has advanced in this space and can help provide a more fair and easily accessible picture of your creditworthiness. For example, collections accounts that have been paid off and hard credit inquiries for credit card applications done within a fourteen-day "rolling" window are less detrimental to your score.

A hard inquiry is what a lender uses to check your score. It can have a negative effect, whereas a soft inquiry is a similar act but will not hurt your score. You will want to ask a lender if they use this method if your credit is an issue. It may provide you with a better report.

The breakdowns for the most recent version of VantageScore (4.0) are as follows:

- **Total Credit Usage, Balance, and Available Credit:** Extremely Influential
- **Credit Mix and Experience:** Highly Influential
- **Payment History:** Moderately Influential
- **Age of Credit History:** Less Influential
- **New Accounts:** Less Influential

LendingTree breaks down the quality of scores on its website like this:

FICO:

Credit Ratings	Credit Scores	Impact on Applicant
Poor credit	300 to 579	May be required to pay a fee or deposit or may not be approved for credit at all.
Fair credit	580 to 669	Considered a subprime borrower who may have difficulty repaying debt.
Good credit	670 to 739	Not considered likely to become seriously delinquent in the future.
Very good credit	740 to 799	Likely to receive better than average rates from lenders.
Exceptional credit	800 to 850	Likely to receive the best rates from lenders.

VantageScore:

Credit Ratings	Credit scores	Impact on Applicant
Very poor credit	300 to 499	Not likely to be approved for credit.
Poor credit	500 to 600	May be approved for some credit, though interest rates may be high and larger down payments may be required.
Fair credit	601 to 660	May be approved for credit without competitive rates.
Good credit	661 to 780	Likely to be approved for credit with competitive rates.
Excellent credit	781 to 850	Most likely to receive favorable rates and terms on credit accounts.

Lowry also provides advice related to your credit. She says, "Your goal should be to join the ranks of the 700+ club... The 700+ club tells lenders you have a history of making wise choices when given access to credit and you make your payments on time." Imagine lending money to someone. You would hope they make wise choices with it and eventually pay you back.

I believe credit is somewhat of a necessary evil. It is not something that you want to rely on, but it is important to have. Lowry also mentions, "Having a strong credit score is like having an insurance policy. You don't want to use it, but it can help prevent a world of financial pain when you need it to." We'll dive more into insurance in the next chapter.

Here are some tips to joining and staying in the 700+ club:

1. Pay your bills on time and pay balances in full.
2. Keep your credit utilization levels low by paying down balances, asking for credit increases (preferably without a hard inquiry), and keeping lines of credit open (even if you don't use them).
3. Check for errors.
4. Use a secured card to start building. This is a credit card that is backed by a cash deposit which lets you avoid traditional underwriting and credit inquiries. Pay your balance in full as with an unsecured card.
5. Use autopay features.

PAYING OFF DEBT

Lowry's advice related to credit cards is strong. "The right way to use a credit card is simple. Don't charge more than you can afford to pay it off every single month. Then, pay it off." Seems pretty easy. Yet, things come up and you have to adjust. If you have debt, it's not something to let you down. It's something that should be addressed, but you can do it.

Two main ways to tackle your debt are the avalanche and snowball methods.

The avalanche method is most mathematically sound, and the snowball method is a more psychologically rewarding way to handle your debt. Each of them requires you to list your debts, except the order is different.

In the avalanche method, you list from the largest to the smallest interest rate. Here's an example:

You have 4 debts.

1. $6,000 owed, $100 minimum monthly payment, 25 percent APR
2. $750 owed, $50 minimum monthly payment, 15 percent APR
3. $2,000 owed, $25 minimum monthly payment, 12 percent APR
4. $600 owed, $25 minimum monthly payment, 5 percent APR

You must pay the minimum on each debt, but you accelerate the payoff on the first one (the one with the highest interest rate). Each would be considered a non-discretionary expense for budgeting purposes. Let's assume you have $500 of excess per month. The minimum monthly payments of debts two to four add up to $100. The remaining $400 would go toward the first debt. Interest would still accrue as you are paying, and it would take a year to eliminate it. Once it's eliminated, you apply the $400 toward the next debt and pay it off at a faster pace. Once that one is paid off you move on to the third.

In total, you would pay $1,787.73 of interest over 23 monthly payments on $9,350 of debt.

In the snowball method, you list from the smallest to the largest amount owed. The second step is the same. You add the minimum payments of the second through fourth debts to your budget as non-discretionary line items and you pay the rest that you have available ($325 out of $500) to the first debt. It would only take two months to pay off item number one.

1. $600 owed, $25 minimum monthly payment, 5 percent APR
2. $750 owed, $50 minimum monthly payment, 15 percent APR
3. $2,000 owed, $25 minimum monthly payment, 12 percent APR
4. $6,000 owed, $100 minimum monthly payment, 25 percent APR

In total, you would pay $2,346.30 in interest over twenty-four monthly payments on $9,350 of debt. Here you would gain psychological momentum by eliminating the initial debts faster, but you'd paid more over a longer period of time.

The avalanche eliminates the high-interest rates first. Those debts cost you the most.

The snowball builds momentum by eliminating items on your list faster. It feels better early on.

Once, again the option you choose needs to be the best for you. Some prefer to know they are not paying as much in interest, others like the feeling of eliminating items better. As long as you are making progress, it's good.

Sites like Financial Mentor, Nerd Wallet, and Undebt.it provide the technology and financial calculators to make it easier to figure out the numbers.

THE MULTIPLIER

The flexibility of debt and the system as a whole are extremely powerful. Some people are made bankrupt because of borrowing and others are made rich. It has a multiplying effect. Wise decisions will ensure it's for your good.

Avoid the costliest debt (like payday loans) if possible. Most people will need to borrow money as an official and legitimate business transaction at some point in their life (the best example is a home mortgage). If that applies to you, it pays to understand the details of the transaction. The same is true even if you are in the position of the lender.

Just like Jerry Jones experienced, overpayment for something special is good. But overpayment for something not so special could really hurt you. There are plenty of tools to assist you in making solid evaluations of borrowing situations. You can use your phone to easily find a mortgage calculator, check property values, look up interest rates, and find reviews of different credit cards.

In your social feed, you will find that mortgage companies will advertise how low their interest rates are and credit card companies boasting about their great perks. Be careful, as the initial interest rate of your loan on an adjustable mortgage is likely to rise significantly. Similarly, the promotional rate of your new credit card will not last forever, and the perks can *never* outweigh the amount of money you are paying for things and any costs you incur for using the card.

Don't let irresponsible borrowing let you feel like a million bucks. You can control this.

There are certain hazards that you cannot control. The next chapter will cover how to handle those types of scenarios.

11.

A Day Late and a Dollar Short

YOU NEED INSURANCE, BORING!

Many dangers in life are impossible to see. Tragedy is often unexpected and unpreventable. However, we should do our best to avoid the situations that we can. Certain risks can be completely avoided. For example, if you're not training properly, it would not be a good idea to go skydiving. Others are not as easily eliminated and there is no social technology that will provide absolute protection. Many people have to drive their car these days. You could choose to never get into a car, but it's more likely you'd take that risk and find a way to mitigate any repercussions.

Insurance can help protect you from major financial problems. In some cases, it's worth it to give up a little to prevent a bigger loss.

HAMMERIN' HANK

It was black history month (February) in 2021. Major League Baseball (MLB) fans would celebrate a little bit differently this year. Henry Louis Aaron passed away on January 22, 2021. Most know him as Hank, and many still consider him the "Home Run King." Aaron was a model of consistency over a career that lasted from 1954 until 1976. He never hit more than forty-seven home runs in a single season but finished his career with 755 and on top of the all-time list.

Aaron experienced terrible racism but was known for being very positive during his home run chase to pass Babe Ruth (He was the leader at the time. He's now third). He will always be remembered for his batting prowess, but also for his ability to see the best in people. He took a risk every time he stepped out onto the field. In fact, he was assigned a bodyguard due to the many death threats he experienced.

One of the threats to Hank read, "You are not going to break his record established by the great Babe Ruth if I can help it. Whites are far more superior than [slur]... My gun is watching your every black move." The bodyguard didn't guarantee Aaron's safety, but it was worth the expense for additional protection.

Thankfully, Aaron went on to play a full twenty-three-year career in Major League Baseball. The death threats did not pan out, but I am sure they caused much fear for Hank and his wife at the time, Billye.

Hank was one of the most famous athletes of his era and was compensated well. His highest salary was in 1975 and 1976 where he earned $240,000. If adjusted for inflation, this is about $1 million per year. That's not nearly as high as the highest-paid baseball players of today.

In February of 2021, Trevor Bauer signed a contract that was worth over $100 million and that pays him about $40 million this year alone (this was prior to being accused of sexual assault later in the year). Needless to say, one year of earning will more than provide for Trevor and his family.

Hank and his family weren't in quite the same situation in the 1970s. If something happened to him, his family's financial situation would have been different. There would be no way to eliminate the pain and suffering of the loss of his life, but a life insurance policy could have provided some financial relief if tragedy struck.

It's best for you to acquire coverage and most likely an insurance company would agree to provide it prior to any conditions that might indicate your mortality is closer than the average person. In a public figure's case, it could be death threats. For most of us, pre-existing medical conditions could prevent us from qualifying. It stresses the importance of making sound long-term planning decisions and getting insured prior to that type of situation.

Aaron's health and longevity helped him to the top of the home run list. He held the MLB career home run record for thirty-three years, three months, and thirty days.

THE NEXT HOME RUN LEADER

On August 7, 2007, Barry Bonds hit his 756th career home run. Hank was surpassed by another African American man. While Barry didn't experience the same depth of racism Hank did, he did (and still does) receive much criticism. Barry played in the "steroid" era of baseball. MLB considers his home runs totally legitimate, but he will always be questioned for his use of performance-enhancing drugs. His career was certainly not without controversy, but his talent was undeniable.

During the height of his career, the majority of which was with the San Francisco Giants, Barry was the most feared hitter in baseball. Some would consider him the most feared of all time. Perhaps the best example of this happened on May 28th, 1998.

Giants manager Dusty Baker decided to rest Barry in the team's home game against the Arizona Diamondbacks that day. It was an otherwise routine Thursday night in MLB. In the bottom of the eighth inning (the home team bats in the bottom of an inning), Dusty pinch hit for Chris Jones with Bonds. The Giants had already scored two runs in the inning to bring the score to 7–5. The Diamondbacks manager, Buck Showalter, brought in relief pitcher Gregg Olson. Olson promptly walked Bonds, but eventually got out of the inning without the Giants scoring anymore.

The Diamondbacks scored in the top of the ninth to make the score 8–5. In the bottom of the ninth, the Giants' last chance to tie the game, they had scored one run already when Barry was up again. The difference this time was the bases were loaded. Bonds could easily have tied or won the game with a base hit, no less a home run, which would have been a grand slam seeing as the bases were loaded.

Olson was still on the mound and it was likely he would be careful pitching to the Giants' star slugger. He didn't have much room for error. He was the team's trusted closer—their best relief pitcher usually called on to finish games. However, that season he pitched 68.2 innings total and appeared in sixty-four games. This shows he typically didn't pitch more than one inning per game. Showalter decided to keep him in the game, nonetheless.

What happened next was unprecedented in the modern record books (there are other instances from 1944 and earlier, but statistical data was not official back then). Olson was ordered to intentionally walk Bonds. Bonds is the career leader in intentional bases on balls (688, second is Albert Pujols with just 312!), but none of them had come with the bases loaded. Showalter was willing to give the Giants a run and bring the tying run to third base (winning to second) to avoid giving Barry a chance to win the game with one swing. That was an incredibly controversial decision and, although it's not that glamorous, it showed a tremendous amount of respect for Bonds.

Giants' catcher Brent Mayne, who coincidentally also pinch-hit to enter the game in the eighth after Bonds did the same, was up next. Mayne worked the count to full (three balls and two strikes) and in a breathtaking moment, hit a solid line drive to right field that was misjudged and almost dropped by the Diamondbacks' Brent Bredde.

The Diamondbacks won the game. There was nothing that the eventual all-time homerun leader could do about it. Buck Showalter made quite a decision to walk Bonds intentionally in that situation. He would have been heavily criticized had Mayne got a hit in the ninth, but he was willing to take the biggest risk off the table. It wasn't a guarantee to work, but he chose to reduce his teams' overall exposure by paying a small price.

It would be great to predict the future. Fear is often manifest in the unknown. It's also an uncomfortable conversation to talk about what you fear, but if you don't talk about it, you'll never be able to address risks of your fears coming true.

Insurance is one of the most complex and avoided aspects of our economic system. It requires predicting the future and talking about what we fear. When was the last time you reviewed your homeowner's or renter's insurance? In the previous chapter, PMI was mentioned. This can required by banks, and it's not something that's enjoyable to research. I've also known many people to simply choose the least expensive health or car insurance because it costs less on a monthly basis and it's easier. Each is also essentially required.

Insurance is a key part of a financial plan. In many ways, we've already identified this through our establishment of an emergency fund. This money is there to ensure you can pay your bills in the case of income loss or for unexpected expenses.

MEDICAL INSURANCE

Insurance is not exciting, but it protects against disaster. It's also not necessary in every situation. You don't have to insure your toe in case you stub it, but if you break your leg and have to go to the hospital, that's not an expense you want to pay out of pocket.

According to Costhelper, the average emergency room cost can be from $150–$3,000. An unexpected expense at that rate could really hurt your budget. If it's a more critical situation, you may find yourself paying a bill in the $20,000 range. Most people are not prepared to take on that expense.

Ehealth reported that in the United States in 2020, the national average premium for medical insurance was $448 per month for a single person and $1,041 per month for family coverage. That is about $12,000 per year for a family.

One big emergency could cost you more than your insurance and your copay for a year.

A copayment is an amount of money that you also have to pay in addition to what your insurer does for a covered service. There are many varieties of copayments, but make sure you are aware of them when calculating your costs in any situation.

Please also be aware of coinsurance, which is an amount of money (often expressed as a percentage) that you must pay toward your care even after your copayment and deductibles. A deductible is a sum of money you are responsible to pay prior to your insurer providing payment. You would pay the coinsurance percentage on all applicable procedures (your insurer paying the rest) until reaching your out-of-pocket maximum. Here is an example:

You need a minor surgery with a total cost of $200.
Your copay is $50.
Your deductible is $500.
Your coinsurance is 80/20, meaning the insurer covers 80 percent and you cover 20 percent (after your deductible has been met).
Your out-of-pocket maximum for your family is $16,000 for the year.

In this scenario you would have to pay the copay of $50 and the ENTIRE $200 for the surgery ($250) total). This is because you must reach your deductible prior to your insurer paying anything. You would have paid $200 toward your $500 deductible. A month later, a member of your family has an accident and requires care that costs $800. Now you would pay the $50 copay (sometimes copays are waived after meeting the deductible), the remaining $300 ($500 - $200 from your surgery, assuming your copay does *not* count toward your deductible—they may) of your deductible, and 20 percent of what's left of the cost of care, which is $100 (0.2x$500). You would pay $150 total. That's actually less than your surgery, which was only one-quarter of the cost ($200) of your family member's care ($800). The insurer would pay their 80 percent responsibility of $400.

If someone in your family had a catastrophic injury and needed a major surgery, you may push up against your out-of-pocket maximum for the year ($16,000). At that point, costs would be completely covered. Although it is currently prohibited, some policies also used to have a lifetime coverage limit. If you ever reached that point, you would be responsible for all costs. Make sure you are aware of this if laws change.

Health insurance in particular is a need for just about everyone in today's society. The stats from 1970–2019 are staggering. According to Health System Tracker, the average person had $353 of annual medical expenses in 1970. In 2019, the amount was $11,582 per year! That's more than thirty-two times more. Total spending was $74.1 billion in 1970 and $3.8 trillion in 2019, an increase of over 512 times. Prices have inflated, but it's clear medical costs are not something to risk.

BEATING CANCER, FINANCIALLY

In 2001, I was diagnosed with cancer. It was completely unexpected in an otherwise well-conditioned teenage athlete. My family was surprised, devastated, and confused. We had no idea what to do. I am sure my parents would have spent any amount of money to get me the treatment I needed, but truthfully, they didn't have enough cash to pay for the consultations, surgeries, and drugs I needed. Thankfully, I was insured under my father's health insurance plan we had through his employer.

It seems there are more and more young people being diagnosed with major illnesses these days, but I was an outlier. The insurance was in place to prevent financial catastrophe for our family in an unlikely situation like the one we found ourselves in. This will not happen to most families, but it could happen to any family. Knowing the insurance would cover the vast majority of the medical bills enabled my parents to concentrate on making important medical and living decisions.

Insurance will not prevent disaster, but it provides financial relief in many cases. In those situations, you'll still experience stress, but if properly insured, you'll be able to handle the resulting financial burden. Major medical insurance is just one of many forms.

IDENTIFYING RISKS

Homeowners or renters insurance provides when there is a disaster to your home and possessions. Flood insurance provides when surging waters damage your home. Life insurance provides for your family if you die. Disability insurance provides if you're hurt or sick and can't work. Long term care insurance provides when you are unable to take care of yourself for mental or physical reasons. Umbrella insurance provides additional coverage over other policies. This is not an exhaustive list of forms of insurance, but it does illustrate that there are many forms of protection.

Not all forms of coverage are for everyone. Just like investments, each person and family's situation are unique. What makes the subject different is there are often shortcomings because of neglect and lack of interest. Yet, it's more devastating to have what is ordinary taken away than it is to not have what's extraordinary. Protect what you have before acquiring more.

To address the risks that apply to you, you must take the time to evaluate your specific scenario. Think about what is most important, and it will be easier to identify the appropriate strategies to implement.

The challenge to making wise insurance decisions is somewhat antithetical to those previously mentioned. Instead of suppressing urges to buy something you want (as some of the other topics in this book), insurance requires consideration of what you don't want. You have to make yourself consider something, rather than trying to avoid thinking about it.

You must acknowledge the risks to you before you can eliminate or lessen them. When you are able to, it provides much motivation to find a mitigation strategy. Insurance often does not completely eliminate risks or your fear of them, but it provides a much more predictable outcome and balance in a given scenario.

The first thing you must determine is what are your most dangerous perils. What things would cause the most devastating financial problems to you and your family? Some common examples are:

- death
- loss of employment due to injury
- auto accident
- medical care (as outlined above)
- damage to your home

Not many people enjoy talking about these things. However, they are just a little easier to deal with if the related financial problems are mitigated. Be sure to consider any dangers specific to you and your family. You may travel a lot, have a profession with extra risk (i.e., logging, aviation, construction, or law enforcement), or rely heavily on a certain part of your body (i.e., musicians, models, surgeons).

It makes sense to talk about the risks before a disaster happens. The biggest should be addressed first and most completely. Financially, it's wise, it provides peace of mind now, and provides clarity later. The previously listed forms of insurance can provide financial protection in case of many well-known disasters.

Perhaps it's some of the stranger insurance policies that illustrate the need for protection. Famous comedy duo Bud Abbott and Lou Costello once took out an insurance policy on their comedy routine "Who's On First?" If something ever caused them to split and they couldn't perform the routine, they would have suffered a significant loss of income. It was the main source of their stardom, and therefore there was a strong isolated risk related to it.

I am sure not being able to perform their routine wasn't something they ever planned or wanted to think about, but Abbott and Costello felt the need to take a preventative measure. You might argue that it would give them a license of irresponsibility knowing that even if the routine couldn't go on, they'd still get paid. The policy also never paid anything because nothing happened during the five-year period it was active. However, it was an important financial decision made at the time of purchase.

Two more examples of unique insurance policies come from the entertainment industry as well. Keith Richards of the Rolling Stones insured his guitar playing abilities and Bruce Springsteen (along with other singers) have insured their voices. We can assume stars of this magnitude would have plenty of money if they could no longer perform. However, it's still worth ensuring they will be compensated even if they can't. They are willing to give up a little to make sure they "win" in the end.

Your situation may not involve superstar amounts of money, but your risks could reach beyond your financial life. Bruce and Keith will be able to pay the bills if they can't perform anymore. But if you are hurt and can't work, who's going to support your family? Queue the AFLAC Duck.

PROFESSIONAL ASSISTANCE
Once you've identified the types of insurance you'll need, assess the options. It's best to work with a professional who understands the type of coverage for which you are looking. They will be able to explain the nuances of the different types of policies and have the computing technology to compare and evaluate different options and projections.

It's also advised to engage highly rated companies. This is important because they are the most likely to keep the contracts to which they agree. There are many rating services, but A.M. Best, Fitch, Moody's, and Standard and Poor's are the most well-known. They measure an insurer's solvency, financial strength, and ability to pay its claims. You want to do business with a solvent and strong company that will be able to pay you in the event you file a valid claim.

As with any product or service, you will find various companies advertising different insurance products across all platforms. Most of them are fitting for somebody, but none of them is the right fit for everyone.

Similar to other items in this book (like credit cards), companies will sell the perks that come with their coverage. They are nice to have, but no perk outweighs the fit of the coverage to your situation. You must evaluate what specific things are covered (and which are not), what all the costs are, and for how much money you are insured.

Don't purchase a policy solely because of a spousal discount, a safe driver discount, a slick mobile application, automatic payments, a recognizable mascot, a memorable jingle, or any other ancillary benefit. There should be no shortcutting or timesaving moves when making a decision.

Many companies will use modern technology for online applications and simple underwriting, which is the process by which an insurer evaluates the risk you would be to cover (similar to a lender's evaluating the risk you present as a borrower from Chapter 10). Ultimately, it determines if they will offer you coverage and at what price. Faster is generally better for them, but not necessarily for you. *This* time doesn't equal money. Don't let speed dictate your decisions. Statistically, it will not affect you, but on the off chance you get in an accident or have a teenage cancer patient in the family, you'll be happy you took the time to choose the right option for you and your family.

Do your best to avoid disaster, but if you can't guarantee you'll avoid it, find a means of protecting yourself. Consider giving up one run to avoid yielding four, like Buck Showalter. You can pay a small amount to prevent being responsible for a devastating sum. Don't end up a day late and a dollar short.

12.

Penny Wise and Pound Foolish

DECISIONS, TAXES, RETIREMENT, AND MORE DECISIONS

What good is it to set up the perfect budget for you and your family only to spend foolishly with what you've saved? There were plenty of times I could have broken open my blue piggy bank and spent my life's savings ($5?) on something worthless.

The challenging thing about discipline in your financial life is it can quickly go for naught with misinformed major decisions. Most of us will always have the possibility of buying something out of our "price range." According to Investopedia, Elon Musk spent $100 million to start SpaceX. I'm pretty sure that would wipe out most people's net worth.

Having your budget in order is supposed to lead to further wise decisions that will put you in a comfortable position as life goes on. Different stages of life have new important financial items to consider. An early budget leads to a less stressful process as you make choices. However, it does not give you a license to "wing" it.

DECISION FATIGUE AND THE UNEXPECTED

I believe the mental work needed to make the correct decisions related to more advanced strategies is harder than that of foundational financial premises. What starts as an effort and discipline-heavy process morphs into something more research-oriented and philosophical.

I suggest understanding the options you have in any situation, researching the benefits and shortcomings of each, and developing a plan even prior to having any decisions to make. The reason for this relates to decision fatigue.

In my work over the years with individuals and families, I've seen unexpected events cause failure to make decisions and lead to numerous undesirable financial situations. None of the choices were overly challenging to make. It was simply the volume of needed decisions in a short period of time that caused the issues. There were usually a few major financial items and many others that weren't even related to money.

If you avoid choices, you can bring on undue financial stress and make yourself susceptible to errant decisions when they are actually made. Dr. Daniel Crosby (previously mentioned in Chapter 7) mentioned in his book *The Behavioral Investor*, "The average investor loses 13 percent of their IQ during financial duress." It's best to avoid this compounding scenario and limit the number of important decisions you could have to make in a short period of time.

You may not be able to prevent the unexpected, but much financial stress can be avoided with a plan (and some of the insurance concepts from the previous chapter).

THE OVERWHELMED WIDOW

One situation I remember involved a widow. This lady was before retirement age when she unexpectedly lost her husband. Losing your spouse of many years is stressful enough, but all the other things a death can bring tend to pile up. She had to deal with hospital bills, insurance claims, deeds to cars and their home, beneficiaries of his things, funeral arrangements, and of course, her financial situation.

We met shortly after her husband passed, and I could tell she was not doing well. Her friend joined her in the meeting, and I thought it was mostly for moral support. However, looking back, I now think her friend made her come. We took about two hours going over different documents and talking about life and financial decisions. Toward the end, I looked at the list of things we had identified as important, and it was almost a full page long. None of them were terribly challenging decisions, but she had to make them. I believe we agreed to meet a week later once she had time to think about everything.

We never met again.

The widow just couldn't handle everything at once. I figured we'd just "knock them out" and she'd be good to go. I thought this would enable her to grieve her husband and not have to worry about everything else. When in fact, just the thought of making decisions that could last her a lifetime was stressful. I pushed her to make too many too fast.

Mathematically, it made sense to decide everything within a week's time, but it wasn't reasonable. The lady ended up calling me multiple times over the years for things that didn't need to be handled immediately and could have waited. She would have benefited from spreading out the decisions no matter how simple they were.

Computing technology could have told us to pay off her house, where to invest, whether to keep her job, which car to sell, how to handle social security, and plenty of other things. Yet, her brain was too overloaded to choose what the computer said in all of those scenarios. It would've been better to handle one item every month or so. She could have dedicated the mental energy needed to handle a single decision every so often. I know it would have saved her some mental anguish and it also would have put her in a much better financial situation in the years following.

QUALITY OVER QUANTITY

Medical News Today says, "Decision fatigue is a psychological phenomenon surrounding a person's ability or capacity to make decisions."

It assumes the quality of your decision-making lessens as you make large amounts of decisions in a short period of time. The brain gets tired of making important decisions and takes "shortcuts" that may provide a more immediate pleasure, despite the inconsistency with a previous plan.

Decision fatigue is directly related to (and according to some, synonymous with) ego depletion. This is a concept that assumes you have a limited amount of self-control. The pleasure-seeking decision mentioned above could be illustrated by a choice to eat something unhealthy because it tastes good despite knowing it is bad for you. You could say you "lost self-control" and had dessert. It was the decision to have a piece of cake. Perhaps you would have skipped it if you hadn't spent dinner making serious decisions about your business.

It must be noted that the decisions do not have to be directly related. Your final business decisions may have also been impaired, but the relation to what caused the "fatigue" or "depletion" is irrelevant. I noticed this concept repeatedly in my work over the years. As long as you're in the window of time in which your mind is tired, it will be harder to make decisions, and thus, any decision you make will be affected.

So, how do you avoid this? I suppose you could train your brain to have more "decision stamina," or an ability to maintain sustained levels of decision-making quality. This is a legitimate strategy, but it's impossible to determine if your training is sufficient. You don't know all of the decisions you are going to have in the future. You can make some general assumptions based on life stage, locations, medical situations, and employment, but rules change and there will always be unexpected scenarios. You might feel you've dramatically improved your mental stamina, but you won't know if it was enough until you have a series of decisions to make.

It is more effective to form a general philosophy, apply it to financial goals, and anticipate major decisions as much as you can. This gives you a baseline system to apply to your decisions and allows you to spread out your decision-making as much as possible. It's the basis of a financial plan. Had the widow from above had a better understanding of her situation and general philosophy about her money, many of the decisions would've been avoided because there would've been no questions as to what to do. While I couldn't eliminate the choices, I was operating under the assumption that some of the items wouldn't take much brainpower.

Financial decision sprints are not effective. An added benefit to distributing the time between major decisions evenly is that your previous decisions are fresher in your mind. There is enough time for it to rest, but not too much that you forget what you even did.

The plan you develop will allow you to lessen the weight of numerous decisions, or you'll be able to avoid them altogether. This ensures the new mental work you have to do in a given situation is strictly around researching and understanding options. A solid plan will tell you what to do once the variables are determined.

TAX
Each of the financial concepts mentioned so far should be applied to the above logic. There are also many other more specific points that will require good planning.

One of the most important things to consider is taxation. Each system has its own methods of calculating taxes on various things. This topic is an excellent example to illustrate the need for advanced planning. There are numerous types of taxes, rates, rules, exceptions, and strategies. There are many books dedicated to this subject alone.

In my experience, most people see their taxes as something to look back on. They wait until it's time to file to drop off their forms at their accountant's office (or upload them digitally now) or pull up TurboTax (a do-it-yourself tax software) when they get an e-mail in March. In the United States, individual and family tax returns are normally due by April 15 of the year following the year for which you are filing. There are federal taxes, state taxes, and local taxes. Other countries have different ways of separating jurisdictions. In all cases, timing and rates should always be considered when filing. More importantly, you should have an understanding of your situation and a forward-looking plan. Reactionary tax planning is less flexible and more likely to induce decision fatigue.

For example, in the US we have an account called an individual retirement account (IRA). This allows taxpayers (with certain restrictions) to contribute up to a specific amount of money ($6,000 in 2019, 2020, and 2021, and $7,000 if you are age fifty or over) in a given year and deduct the amount from their income for tax purposes. In relation to timing, this is a deferral of taxes. You would not pay tax on the amount you contributed to your IRA in the year you earned it. However, in a "traditional" IRA, in most cases, you will have to pay taxes on the amount you have when you take it out of the account. Generally, you need to be 59.5 years or older to do this without a penalty. Depending on your age, 59.5 could be decades away! That doesn't mean you shouldn't think about it until then.

With the IRA, the Internal Revenue Service (IRS) is promoting long-term and retirement savings by providing upfront tax relief and requiring the money to stay in your account until a more advanced age. In theory, you are saving by avoiding taxes during your earning years and paying them when your income is lower in retirement. With progressive tax brackets (meaning you pay a higher rate on higher levels of income), you would owe a smaller amount later in life.

The traditional IRA is not the best move for everyone. First of all, we don't actually know what tax rates will be in the distant future. In addition to that, some people earn a living but are still in a relatively low tax bracket. The Taxpayer Relief Act of 1997 established the Roth IRA. This was previously a concept proposed by senators Bob Packwood of Oregon and William Roth of Delaware in 1989. It took almost a decade but starting in 1998, taxpayers were allowed to contribute money to a Roth IRA (named after William).

The primary difference between the Roth and its predecessor is the money you put into it does not yield a tax deduction. In other words, you do pay taxes on the money you contribute. However, the money still grows tax-deferred, and you do *not* have to pay taxes on the money when you take it out. This is a significant difference, and the decision to make contributions will have a *huge* effect on what happens when you take the money out years, maybe decades, later.

Here's a comparison of equal amounts of money used in a traditional IRA, a Roth IRA, and an account without qualified tax benefits (a non-qualified investment account) for long-term savings. We will look at just a single amount of money earned for illustrative purposes and use a flat tax rate of 25 percent (as opposed to a progressive model) on the front and backend. We will project a 10 percent annual investment return for simplicity. Ultimately, the rate of return is not relevant to the illustration.

	Amount Earned	Amount Invested	10 Years	20 Years	30 Years	Value after 25% Tax	Value after 15% Tax	Value after 35% Tax
Non-Qualified	$10,000	$7,500	$19,453	$50,456	$130,871	$98,153	$111,240	$85,066
IRA	$10,000	$10,000	$25,937	$67,275	$174,494	$130,871	$148,320	$113,421
Roth IRA	$10,000	$7,500	$19,453	$50,456	$130,871	$130,871	$130,871	$130,871

*25% tax rate at earnings

Note it's possible your income is low enough in thirty years that you don't owe taxes. In that case, the traditional IRA would be a steal because you would pay no taxes (as long as your withdrawals don't push you to a point of owing). Also, it's likely you will have more than one contribution over a thirty-year period. The compounding effect of returns would provide you a higher amount. This is just an example to compare the types of accounts.

As the table illustrates, the tax rate is what matters. If your tax rate is lower in thirty years (15 percent) the traditional IRA wins. If it is higher (35 percent), the Roth IRA wins. In either case, the non-qualified lags because although it assumes no taxable transactions during the thirty years investment period, it is taxed on both ends. If you had made transactions during the investment period, it's likely you'd generate additional tax liability dragging down the value even more.

The decision as to which option to choose is more than a determination on which is the "best" type of account. It would take research into your tax situation and your belief in how the system will work in the future. If you felt like tax rates would be higher in the future, you might choose the Roth. If you felt they'd be lower, that would be a reason to choose the traditional. A combination is also a legitimate strategy. These are things you can have a general idea of prior to the deadline for contributions to IRA's which is normally the date taxes are due for that contribution year (usually April 15 as mentioned above, giving you three and a half months after the year is over to still contribute for that time period).

Plan ahead to avoid decision fatigue. This type of foresight could've helped the widow from above.

In addition to the above income tax example, there are other forms of taxes that need to be considered. Many systems throughout the world also have sales taxes, business taxes, property taxes, and estate taxes (estate planning is addressed in the next chapter) among others. Taxes should never be evaded, but you should take advantage of the rules that benefit you.

THE HOMESTEAD EXEMPTION

An example of a rule designed to benefit local taxpayers is the homestead tax exemption for homeowners. This allows you to exclude a portion of the value of your home from taxation. It is absolutely expected that those who are eligible use the benefit. The government is giving incentives to its citizens for a reason.

It pays to have a knowledgeable tax advisor who has your best interest in mind. They can use comprehensive types of software to make short-term and long-term predictions. You must take your entire situation into account and make informed decisions (often in advance) related to all items. It's not as simple as the single cautionary item mentioned in the tax ad you saw in early April.

There are easily more than fifty tax deductions and credits in the United States. This illustrates the complexity of the system and the need for advanced planning and a sound decision-making process. Policy Genius published a short synopsis of some deductions and credits and IRS.gov provides a detailed breakdown of everything. Tax deductions lower your income prior to calculating how much you owe, and Tax Credits will lower the amount you owe. Non-refundable credits "stop" at "0," and refundable credits will provide you a rebate if they add up to more than you owe.

RETIREMENT PLANS

Another area that carries important decisions and that needs to be addressed way in advance of results is employer-sponsored retirement plans. There are a lot of different ways for employers to structure these. They can provide a nice incentive to work for a company but may also be complex. Taxation is a part of the conversation, and it's advised to set aside specific time with your loved ones and professional advisor to make decisions regarding these plans.

Once again, projection software can be very useful to illustrate multiple scenarios and decision fatigue should be avoided.

Some companies will contribute money to a defined contribution plan for you, and others will match a certain percentage of your own contribution. The exact amount contributed is known (different from the defined-benefit plans mentioned below). The performance of underlying investments is generally not guaranteed. If your employer offers a match, you get additional compensation for just saving some of your money. Pretty nice, huh?

You may have heard of terms such as a 401(k), 403(b), or 457 plans. These are employer-sponsored retirement plans. 401(k)s are generally offered by for-profit companies, 403(b)s by non-profits, and 457s by government institutions.

Alternatively, some employers have what is called a defined-benefit plan. These plans pay you a certain amount at retirement based on a formula related to your income and years of service. In contrast to the defined contribution plan, the amount you receive later is defined. A popular term is a pension plan.

Some plan types for smaller employers or those with startup plans are simplified employee pensions (SEP) and savings incentive match plan for employees (SIMPLE). Still another option for some situations is direct payroll deductions to IRA accounts like those mentioned above.

A company can also benefit its employees by providing a form of ownership in the company. One way to do this is called an employee Stock option plan (ESOP). These plans have a comprehensive set of rules. Stock can be offered in numerous ways and the timing of when it is acquired and sold is important to consider. Again, having a plan will prevent stressed decisions.

Stock can be offered through incentive stock options (ISOs), non-qualified stock options (NSOs), and restricted stock. Each has its own nuances. The first two give an employee the option to buy stock in the company. ISOs can offer a discounted price on the stock and don't trigger a taxable event on exercise. There are potential tax breaks on the profit when sold. NSOs are simpler but don't have the same tax benefits for you. They actually provide a tax deduction for the employer. Restricted stock shares are actual shares at issue but have incentives or lengths of employment that must be met to "unrestrict" the shares. Once again, the tax rules are complicated.

It can be tempting to sell your ISOs quickly (especially if your company is doing well). However, you can save a lot of money by holding on to them. Don't sell them as a reaction without understanding the possible future repercussions. Your plan should consider other sources of money for a purchase prior to that generated from an early sale of stock options.

Eventually, your employer-sponsored retirement plan should become part of your retirement. At that point, you will have more important financial decisions to make. But hopefully, you have a plan that will lessen the burden and avoid decision fatigue.

Previously, your decisions were about where and how to grow your assets. Now, you'll be concentrating on spending. This can be a hard transition. Dr. Wade Pfau is the founder of Retirement Researcher and a professor at the American College of Financial Services. His extensive research shows there is no one best practice for retirement income. He believes, "Determining the sustainable spending rate from a diversified investment portfolio in retirement requires making decisions about longevity and market returns."

How are we supposed to decide about things that are not certain? We can't guarantee anything and that is why a detailed plan that considers your comfort level with the variables is very important. Pfau suggests, "Sometimes people spend more time looking at how to save $20 when they buy the next vacuum cleaner than they do thinking about how they are going to approach a retirement income plan. Some of those decisions can add up to $100,000 or more over the lifetime." It's best to avoid decision fatigue by considering these things well in advance of your actual retirement. When the time comes and your lifestyle changes drastically, you can just implement what you have already determined and concentrate your brainpower on unexpected things and other life decisions.

Some of Pfau's suggestions for planning include:

- Play the long game. —Plan on living a long time. Your money will need to last.
- Use reasonable expectations for portfolio returns. —I believe this relates to any situation. The stock market has returned about 10 percent per year since its inception. You can't assume that's what it will be every year, especially near or in retirement.
- Approach retirement income tools with an agnostic view. —There is a long list of incredibly complex vehicles for retirement assets. A description of each is beyond the scope of this text. There are ads for many. As always, use the technology available for information, not decision-making. Consult a trustworthy professional.

In speaking with Pfau, I learned behavioral bias is an important part of making retirement projections and due to the decumulation aspect of this stage, sequence of returns risk is magnified. He has written, "When spending from a portfolio, the concept of sequence of returns risk becomes more relevant, as portfolio losses early in retirement will increase the percentage of remaining assets withdrawn to sustain an income." You must consider how you will feel when market fluctuations occur. Will you be comfortable adjusting your spend rate? At this point, you will no longer have time on your side. You will be using what you've saved as things happen.

There are many computer programs available that can make retirement projections, but none can predict with accuracy all the variables. Pfau said "a lot of them exist in a black box and some of the assumptions behind them may not be appropriate at all" and "it's hard to know which calculators are doing what." In this case, the technology can be used for assistance but will not make decisions for you.

The Investments and Wealth Institute published a 2017 Study by Greenwald and Associates that said 58 percent of retirees withdraw less than what their investments earn. Pfau also mentioned seeing this in his research but suggested that it may be because of excellent stock market growth over the past decade. What if the market performed poorly for an extended period of time during your spending period?

Understanding your tax situation and retirement plan will go a long way toward the sound management of your long-term savings and the rest of your financial pyramid. The further up the pyramid you go, the more projecting that must be done, and the more unseen variables there are. More variables mean more complexity, which in turn means more decisions.

Financial organizations with retirement products and services use retirement as a lead generation machine. They know that people have major concerns that they haven't thought about until that point. Hiring someone or purchasing a product for retirement is recommended if you don't have any assistance. My suggestion is to consider your situation at least annually at all stages of life and eliminate the heavy burden that many find at the dawn of retirement. Dedicate a little time now with a clear mind and you'll save a lot of effort later.

13.

Bang for Your Buck

ESTATE PLANNING IS HEALTHY

Death is inevitable. I used to avoid conversations about it. However, I've learned they are needed. My earliest memories of the subject are related to the pets I had as a child. Some of them died suddenly, and it was not an ending I could easily accept. It took time, but I was able to get over the sadness.

More recently I have lost people in my life who also meant a lot. In addition to the emotional pain, there have also been legal and financial issues to deal with. It goes without saying, but losing a pet is a much different experience than losing a person.

Although none of us know exactly when we will die, we can do some planning for the more technical aspects of our passing to ease some of the stress it can cause for our families.

Conversations about end-of-life planning are not an exciting topic. It's probably more avoided than the insurance conversations I encouraged you to have in Chapter 11. In many cases, it includes conversations about life insurance, so the subjects certainly overlap. Life insurance can be an important tool to use when planning what your family will receive in the event of your passing.

David Lenok is an attorney, senior editor at wealthmanagement.com, and the host of the *Celebrity Estates: Wills of the Rich and Famous* podcast. He said, "It's a hard conversation to get started, but once you get it started, it's really easy to keep going." The topic is not attractive, but when you realize the importance of the items, you tend to want to complete the planning.

On one hand, it's sensible there isn't much to worry about when thinking about your estate because you will not be around. However, when you think about the stress that can be caused by a death, you might think differently. The emotional pain your loved ones will feel is not preventable and we are all going to pass eventually.

Beyond emotional stress, there are other pain points your family will have to deal with when you die. No situation can be categorized as better or worse, but there are many different scenarios. On one end of the spectrum, if you pass prematurely, there may be debts (like a mortgage) and dependents (children) who rely on your income. You should have a plan to address this. On the other end, you might live a long healthy life, build a business, and accumulate wealth in various forms. Your estate, at that point, could be very complicated and without specific directions, it could cause extreme tension among your heirs.

THE ESTATE THAT KEEPS ON GIVING

Lenok identified the story of Anna Nicole Smith, her husband billionaire J. Howard Marshall, and their estates, a prominent case with good examples of estate planning issues. Smith was twenty-six years old and Marshall was eighty-nine when they were wed. Marshall died just thirteen months later. It seems like your typical "gold digger" scenario, but when you break down some of the conflicts, it could be relevant to anyone.

Smith and her stepson were battling over Marshall's oil fortune, but this sort of conflict can arise regardless of the amount of money involved. Adding to the complication was Smith's unique lifestyle as an actress, model, and exotic dancer. Litigation over the legitimacy of the marriage, and a bankruptcy Smith filed for in 1996 lasted for well over a decade.

The California Bankruptcy Court, the US Court of Appeals for the Ninth Circuit, and the US Supreme Court traded many rulings. Marshall had two kids. One was not listed in his will and filed his own claims against the estate. The other who had been fighting against Smith died in 2006. His widow continued to pursue the case on behalf of his estate.

Then, in 2007, Smith was found dead in a hotel room, which set off a whole different set of arguments. The case was then on behalf of Smith's infant daughter who was the only child of hers alive at that point. Her son died while visiting her in the hospital just a few days after she gave birth to his half-sister.

Smith's will had a clause that disinherited any children she may have after writing it, including any children she may not know that she had. That is about as bizarre as it gets. Lenok posed a possible explanation that it was some sort of default clause that a man might use that was accidentally left in Smith's documents.

The lesson to be learned from this example is this should be a very detailed process. The smallest of language adjustments could cause years of litigation and millions of dollars. The celebrity nature of the case and the compilation of events are not things that most will have to deal with, but the individual situations are all not so rare. Lenok stresses that once you get past the "silly surface part," the blended family disagreements are the same problem for everyone. People can be brought together by one person, and when that person is no longer around, they are bound to disagree on certain things.

I provide this example not as a threat, but to highlight how when you are not around can make handling your responsibilities and possessions very challenging. If you are looking for a good example of a more well-formed celebrity estate plan, see actor and comedian Robin Williams'. He died by suicide and theoretically it would have been easier to plan because he knew when he would die. More importantly, though, the structure and legal details provide some great insight. There's no way to truly grade an estate plan, but it was well prepared. It likely reduced the stress his loved ones felt and certainly made the legal process easier.

Talking about your own death may not be a conversation you desire, but it's one to be had. Privacy can be a big concern for most people. Without the proper documents, your estate will be subject to probate which is the public process of proving a will. You may want to use other estate planning tools to shield your assets from the public eye upon your death. It's not likely to rise to Anna Nicole Smith's publicity, but most families would want to have as little as possible available for mass consumption.

Decision fatigue can make another appearance when forming even the most basic of estate plans. My suggestion is to address things incrementally as needed to avoid adverse choices when your brain is tired from making intense decisions. Lenok also stressed the need to just start the conversation.

Many sources will suggest at least these three foundational estate planning documents:

1. Last Will and Testament—indicates how you want your property distributed, appoints an executor (the person who carries out the wishes you've indicated) of your estate, and a contingent.
2. Durable Power of Attorney (PoA)—enables someone to make legal and financial decisions on your behalf.
3. Advance Medical Directive/Living Will/Health Care Power of Attorney (HCPA)—indicates healthcare decisions you desire in the case of your incapacity or gives someone the power to make decisions for you.

Laws vary by country and state, but the relevant form of these items can all be acquired by working with an estate planning attorney or reputable firm.

TRUSTS

In addition to the above documents, some situations call for a revocable living trust. These are used for various reasons including directing assets, privacy, minimizing estate taxes, and avoiding probate. Probate is the legal process of settling a will through the court system. It can be expensive and time-consuming.

Revocable living trusts are not the only type of trusts. In fact, there are numerous types, and depending on the complexity of your situation, you may need more than one. Once again, work with an estate planning attorney (consult multiple to determine who you are comfortable with) to meet your needs.

Outside of special documents, you'll want to make sure that any accounts you own have the desired beneficiaries listed. Usually, these types of things don't have to be directed in a will or to a trust. They can be, but if you just want your retirement account to go to your spouse, all you have to do is contact the provider and make sure that he or she is listed as the primary beneficiary. You'll also want to list a contingent in the case of them predeceasing you or a simultaneous death.

One of the most stressful things related to working closely with families and their finances is uncertainty. It's very hard to prepare for the future you do not know what it will bring.

Estate planning is aptly named what it is instead of estate projecting or estate guessing. In my experience, the thoroughness of a plan is directly negatively correlated to the stress level (and not just financial) a family experiences at the loss of a loved one.

THINK ABOUT REALITY AND YOUR HEIRS

I have seen people of various levels of financial wealth pass away unexpectedly and with forewarning. When the deceased had at least prepared the foundational documents, decisions were limited and much easier. General fatigue can set in quickly for a family, and decision fatigue is only exacerbated. I experienced time-sensitive decisions that failed to be made (the overwhelmed widow from the previous chapter is just one example), and others rushed without reason. If nothing else, a little bit of planning now can make things that much easier for your family when your time comes.

If you'd like to take some extra steps to make a detailed plan, I recommend incorporating as many people as you can in the process. They all don't need to know exactly what items they are to receive or amounts of money, but you can alert them what your intentions are. You can make sure everyone understands the plans and that they will work together. No one wants an estate with a dispute and fighting heirs.

In his book *Splitting Heirs*, Ron Blue lists five straightforward realities:

1. We will all die.
2. We will take nothing with us.
3. We will probably die at a time other than we would like.
4. Someone else will get our stuff.
5. We can only decide before we die who gets our stuff after we die.

Ron outlines all the decisions that need to be made within an estate plan. The vast majority of them are not assisted by modern technology. Services like LegalZoom, LegalShield, and Trust and Will can speed up the document creation process, but they do not replace the mental efforts needed to decide what happens when you are gone. The technology of an organization like Vanilla offers a more robust process. Yet, it's still advised to have some traditional contemplation and conversation despite the intimidation of the above list.

Lenok also stressed this should not be a set-and-forget event. I have seen a lot of people use digital estate planning services and fail to reference the documents through many life changes. Some will address their plan as they get older and make the time to adjust things. However, others may forget or pass prematurely. In which case some undesirable outcomes can arise. If you are led to an online estate planning service and that gets the conversation going and provides value for what you need at the time, I would encourage it. Just make sure you consult a professional person as things get more complex and you need to make updates.

It has been said more people fear public speaking than death. This could be true but talking about your own demise is not always an enjoyable conversation. It can be tough but should not be put off. It lessens the chances your desires will be met and makes your loved ones suspect to decision fatigue during a tough time.

A 2021 report by caring.com stated that just 32.9 percent of adults in the United States have a will. This is down from 42 percent in 2017. There are other forces that could be at play, such as the pandemic and a large nu mber of people becoming adults, but it's not a good sign from a planning perspective.

Interestingly, young adults (age eighteen to thirty-four) were more likely to have an estate planning document than middle-aged adults (thirty-five to fifty-four). The older you are, the closer you are to death, and the more complex your situation can be. Either way, any encouragement to start the process is good, whether it's a digital ad, a personal solicitation from an estate planning attorney, or just a self-induced family conversation.

The fear of death or the process of dying is known as thanatophobia. Planning your estate may not eliminate this fear but talking about how you would like to benefit your heirs and making sure they are protected at your passing can be a nice process. It can provide comfort and a sense of accomplishment. It can bring your family together and provide a reason to celebrate some of the great things in your life. It can also provide an opportunity for teaching and learning moments among generations.

Looking forward by looking back is a very healthy exercise. Think about the great things you have done so far and the impactful legacy you can leave for future generations. If you understand where you've been, you can share great things with future generations. You will get more bang for your buck. Estate planning can help you do this.

14.

Worth Its Weight in Gold

HOW A LOVE OF GENEROSITY IS PERSONAL

They say in giving, you receive. This is true, but what is often mistaken is the amount you give is correlated to the amount you receive. You don't have to give $1,000,000 to a charity to feel like a million bucks.

Philanthropy has an unfortunate aura because it is generally measured in dollars. Americans gave $449.64 billion in 2019. This reflects a 5.1 percent increase from 2018. Those are staggering numbers, but I think it's more impressive that in 2020 giving grew by 2 percent. That means despite all the financial hardships many people and businesses went through, we still gave more than we had in previous years.

One reason for charitable giving is it often provides the donor with a tax deduction. There are legitimate strategies to take advantage of the rules. However, it's strictly anecdotal but I have surmised we are most generous in times of need. There is a natural human inclination to support people who are struggling. It doesn't matter if you are in a less desirable position than you have been in the past. People supported other people in 2020. The tax break was an ancillary benefit.

MAKING A MEANINGFUL DIFFERENCE

Your giving is meaningful when you make a noticeable difference. Its effectiveness is *not* tied to a specific amount of money. There are no minimums. It's about the mindset and is a deeply personal experience. In thirteen years of having charitable conversations with people, I have seen all kinds of different ways for people to express themselves. Some give their money. Some give time. Others use their talents to benefit others. Within those groups, some people give spontaneously while others are very planned. There is no right way, but your way.

The desire to help other people is inherent. Human nature is to provide, whether it is for our family or other people. The joy you feel when you help another person can be hard to describe. It's different than the feeling you get when eating, exercising, doing something fun, or working. Each of those can feel good, but they are not the same as caring for another human. With that in mind, consider a huge sum of money would not make everyone happy or even solve their problems. In fact, significant financial wealth has been known to cause more problems.

NOT YOUR TYPICAL TRIP TO MEXICO

I have had the opportunity to travel overseas multiple times to serve families in need with an organization known as

Habitat for Humanity. They have a great handle on the housing, water, and sanitation needs of impoverished families throughout the world. They make it easy for volunteers and donors to help a major cause without having to spend a lot of time researching and preparing. You can bring a team together rather quickly and head to a foreign land and chip in. You also don't need a lot of experience.

On one of my trips, we had the pleasure of serving in an indigenous Mayan community in Mexico. The community we served on this particular trip was so isolated they did not speak the language of the country in which they lived. It was far from any city and communication was primarily verbal. Their language, called Tzotzil, was not written or distributed anywhere else.

One day, we were working pretty hard on the family's new home when it was time for a break. The sun was beating down and the humidity was 100 percent. The group of about fifteen people headed over to the tent where the water was. We must have drunk a few gallons in five minutes. Most of us were complaining about the heat when someone on the team yelled out, "I love this!" We all looked up and smiled. It was a simple message, but a great reminder of why we were there. The break ended and we got back to work.

Everyone got back to working really hard, but I was somewhat distracted. If you've experienced my persona on one of these build sites, it's normally anything but distracted. It's amazing how engaged and energetic you can be doing physical labor when it's for a good cause. It was obvious I wasn't thinking right.

After a few minutes of experiencing my altered state, one of the Habitat employees named Sebastien came over to me. He was the only person who wasn't a member of the community we were in who spoke Tzotzil fluently. He also spoke broken English. Through some hand gestures and stumbling through words, he was able to ask me what was wrong. I said, "nothing." I explained I was overwhelmed.

I knew I had invited this group of people to a foreign country with a tropical climate to do incredibly challenging and unfamiliar physical labor for a family they didn't even know. What was I thinking? I was trying to do something great, and for a moment I thought I had done something pretty dumb. I thought the break we just had was a demoralizing chance to escape the pain. I was wrong.

One of our teammates yelled, "I love this!" Suddenly, I felt this amazing sense of joy. Everyone smiled, and that moment seemed to validate the whole trip. Anything could have happened beyond that point, and I still would have been overjoyed.

I was moved by how much everyone *loved* the trip. Love is a powerful thing. It's one word with so much meaning. Or is it? It's up to eight different words, if you speak Greek (still powerful, though).

Once I was able to express what I was thinking to Sebastien, he smiled. I think we even had a cement and dirt-filled embrace. We were about to head back to work when I realized I needed more than Sebastien to understand how I felt.

One of the great things about these experiences is you develop amazing relationships with the families you work with. It was important I told the family the team's love for the experience. I took Sebastien over to one of the family members. She was a teenage girl who actually spoke a few English words and was often involved in translating throughout the week. I had no clue what they were saying to each other, but I assumed it would be a fairly simple interaction. I was wrong. Sebastien paused, looked at me, and explained how he was having trouble explaining how we loved the experience. I said, "What do you mean? Just tell her we love them! Hopefully, they love us back. I know we're a little weird, but we're trying to help." He laughed and there was another pause that seemed like fifteen minutes. Then, Sebastien said, "They have no word for love." I was confused. It didn't make sense. How could you not tell someone you love them?

SHOWING LOVE

After the interaction, I was a little disappointed but more determined to do the best we could for this family that "didn't have love." The week continued to go well, and we finished everything we were supposed to before going home.

It's customary to have a home dedication for the family at the end of a build. As the leader of the trip, it was my job to say a few words (with Sebastien translating) to the entire community and wrap up the week. We would also hear from the family. I didn't think of it beforehand, but I must've said the word "love" ten times in my mini speech. When I finished, I realized what I had done and thought it would have meant nothing to them. I was wrong—again. Are you sensing a theme here?

The young lady to whom I tried to explain my feelings earlier stood up and addressed the crowd. She was confident and beaming with pride. She said a lot in Tzotzil and a little in English. When she finished, she was emotional. Sebastien translated her words in a fraction of the time it took her to say them. He said, "They have felt God's love from you all this week. There is no word for love because it is expressed through action."

Our experience in a small, isolated indigenous community taught me that caring for others is an expression of love. It does not cost money, it is not measured in time, and it is part of every culture in our world.

We're missing something in an era when seeking digital "likes" has become the way we find joy. We want validation from everyone. We see the "best them" on the internet, but we don't actually communicate. Their heart-shaped approval is addicting but fleeting.

GIVING MORE THAN MONEY

Despite the issues, the need to care for others still exists. So, what do we do? We give what we can. We give what fits in the budget. I've stated the budget is important, but that's for financial matters. Unfortunately, we've reduced generosity to a financial matter. Giving money, no matter what we can afford, is not the way to approach this. Human giving is interactive. It's inspiring. It's love.

When giving becomes a part of your life, you find joy. It's a different joy than a tax deduction and it should be a more than sufficient replacement for digital approvals we get from our social applications. Sylvia Brown's (from the *Speaking of Impact* podcast episode referenced in Chapter 7) family has a three-hundred-year history of philanthropic work, and Sylvia has dedicated her life to helping people give. In her work, Brown has learned the hormones induced by giving last about two hours. To make the joy last beyond that, it's not about giving more money. It's about putting a little time and effort into your philanthropy.

I asked Sylvia about people's giving habits. The similarities between the topics of the other chapters were striking. Technology always seems to be the great magnifying glass. It makes everything bigger.

Bigger is not always better. Giving money is so easy now with online giving platforms that people can give to a cause in just a few clicks. Technology makes it really easy—but almost too easy. Brown talked about how people are giving with solely their hearts and not using their heads. Ironically, technology has led us down this path. More time needs to be spent on determining the impact an organization is having because it means they are effective, and it also makes your giving more meaningful.

Charity Navigator and Guidestar are examples of organizations that provide reports and metrics for evaluating charitable organizations. While these are helpful from a technical perspective, Brown stressed it is more important to actually determine the effect of the work that is being done. It's good to know one million meals have been served, but are the hunger or associated health and mortality issues being positively impacted? Look for outcomes over outputs.

THINK BEFORE YOU GIVE

When we were in Mexico, I felt the impact we were making. The benefactors' lives were significantly improved. We continue to experience consistent joy knowing of and following the organization's work. Brown warned against "mixing up activities with impact." There is a tendency to believe that just because an organization is a non-profit that it's using its resources well or actually making the impact you assume. I urge you to participate in a charity's efforts. Don't assume anything.

Brown has a campaign called Think Before You Give. It's designed to assist people in giving wisely and avoiding what she calls "contented apathy." Their hearts are satisfied with giving but they don't actually know the effectiveness of their support and the organizations they gave to as a whole.

Technology seems to be taking the thinking out of giving, leading to people comfortably donating without knowledge of a charity's impact. Brown said 85 percent of donors in the United States spend about fifteen minutes executing their giving. I am not saying you need to take a week-long trip to another country, but this is much less time than people spend on major purchases such as vacations or large appliances. It reminded me of the conversation I had with David Lenok (Chapter 13) about the time people spend on estate planning. It's just not getting the time it deserves.

Brown outlines three criteria to assist people in evaluating causes:

Scale—Will your dollar make a growing difference?

Solvability—Do they address a problem that can be fixed?

Connectedness—How can you be part of the cause?

Thinking about these three things will help you create a "funnel" to filter your options. Brown recommends using these criteria to think deeply about 80 percent of your giving. The remaining 20 percent you can allow for more spontaneous efforts. This mix will allow you to have a more meaningful relationship with your philanthropy and also account for those more urgent times where it's not appropriate to apply a more time-consuming method.

IMPACT IS GREATER THAN MONEY

In conclusion, the modern methods of information and monetary transfers have allowed organizations to communicate and accept donations more freely. This should be celebrated. But when it comes to the impact and fulfillment you experience in giving, it's important you dedicate time to contemplating its effectiveness.

My experience in Mexico was a unique event. However, it made it clear we were making an impact. I know people's lives were made better and I still experience joy in thinking about that time. As a result, I have given more money and spent more time doing that type of work. Ironically, it was being mostly isolated from technology that enabled me to have the experience. Whether it is applying Brown's criteria or physically doing the work of an organization, I encourage you to evaluate the impact of the causes you are considering supporting.

Put down the checkbook, or mobile wallet, and develop a relationship with a cause and the people in need. Your philanthropy will transform into something enjoyable, meaningful, and lasting. Then, you can use the technology to handle the less meaningful tasks like transferring your monthly donation or calculating your tax deduction.

Automating your financial generosity so that you can concentrate on the experience of giving is worth its weight in gold.

15.

Bread and Butter

HOW TO DEVELOP A VISION FOR SUCCESS

There are a lot of great things in life that are easily enjoyed in moderation. A little hot sauce is excellent on your taco. A half-hour of sun on the skin could be a healthy dose of vitamin D. Exercise is great, but you can injure yourself with too much.

Other things in the world aren't so easy to acquire, and we say things like, "If I could just get a taste of it," and, "I would die to try that for just five minutes." I'd love to play just one snap in the Super Bowl, but I know it's not happening. I'd also love to know what it would be like to run a big technology company, like those I've referenced in this book.

The great thing about the financial world is it lets you try things out or even own a piece of a huge company that would be unaffordable for just about everyone on the planet. Review Chapter 7 for more on investing.

While it's possible to buy stock in a great company, the valuable lessons are in the building of something great. Most of us will not end up as famous tech entrepreneurs, but there are great lessons to learn from those who are. They can teach us how to envision our own personal success, ideal lifestyle, and successful financial plan.

The most modern, technologically advanced computer company was founded in 1976. That's forty-five years ago. That's a long time and the world is much different now, but the vision hasn't changed. Apple Computer, Inc (originally Apple Computer Company) shares now hold the largest market capitalization of any stock. It should be noted the sum of all the types of Alphabet, Inc shares would put it at the top of the list. Either way, Apple has worked its way through numerous "seasons" of business and is firmly planted in the top echelon of worldwide organizations.

Apple was founded by Steve Jobs, Steve Wozniak, and Ronald Payne. They each hold an important role in the story of Apple. Jobs was the visionary. Wozniak was the programmer. Payne was the older, wiser, "adult in the room." While Payne's involvement didn't last a year, and Wozniak left in the mid-'80s, Jobs spent many more years carrying out what he "saw."

Forty-five years does not come without struggles. Jobs was known for being a strong personality and hard to work with. In fact, Jobs left Apple in 1985 after a power struggle with the CEO at the time, John Sculley. He wasn't brought back until 1997 when his other company, NEXT, was acquired by Apple.

Jobs' original vision for Apple was, "To make a contribution to the world by making tools for the mind that advance humankind." It was going to be a challenge, but he had a clear and simple idea of what he wanted the company to do. This vision continued to drive him and the company from 1997 until his passing in 2011.

Throughout Jobs' tenure, Apple concentrated on innovation and creating tools that carried out his original vision.

His obsession with innovation is probably best summed up by a quote of hockey legend Wayne Gretzky which Jobs used in his keynote address at Macworld (a trade show style conference for Apple's Macintosh computer) in 2007:

"I skate to where the puck is going to be, not where it has been."

He follows the quote with important words of his own.

"And we've always tried to do that at Apple. Since the very, very beginning. And we always will."

There is no doubt what the intention was. They were going to take the next step. They wanted to innovate.

Perhaps the best measure of resilience is in one's failures. Apple Computer, Inc. has a list of many not-so-successful ventures like the Apple III and Lisa (an early personal computer). Even the original Macintosh wasn't as consistent as expected. Whether Jobs was there or not, they kept pushing on. Their attempt at a video game console (Apple Pippin), personal digital assistant (PDA, Apple Newton), and hybrid laptop/PDA (Apple eMate) all went terribly. However, as Apple continues to innovate, it never loses its vision. Their latest product is the AirTag item tracker (sales began April 30, 2020). AirTags can be attached to other items to keep track of them using the Find My App on Apple's operating system, iOS.

As of August 24, 2011, Tim Cook has been the CEO of Apple. Cook said in reference to Jobs, "His vision for Apple was a company that turned powerful technology into tools that were easy to use, tools that would help people realize their dreams and change the world for the better."

There has been much controversy over Apple's direction since Jobs died but Cook states in that quote the original vision is still alive. It has been driving the company for forty-five years.

There is no way to predict the future in any area of life. Unfortunately, tough times and mistakes are inevitable, but they do not have to be catastrophic. The proper vision allows you to learn from mistakes and push through to reach your goals and make visions a reality. It doesn't matter if you're a multi-billion-dollar company, a young hungry computer technician, or an average family of four.

Financial management can be very technical, but it's not the number-crunching (which technology handles much of these days) that signifies a great system. Just like in business, it's the vision. Every good system has foundational premises drawn from what the creators would like to see in the future.

You must stress the importance of customizing a plan to your own needs. There are many predefined strategies that can provide a good start to developing a plan, and many professionals will draw on the general premises before applying them to specific situations. The specificity should always be defined first.

It's impossible to come up with action points to a plan of any kind without understanding what is desired. A visioning and goal-setting process will lead to that point and provide direction for a plan specific to you.

Visioning involves determining what you would like to see in the future. It can often be a very enjoyable process because there are no incorrect answers, and it empowers you to act. Things you desire move into reach. What may not have ever been thought of as possible becomes something you can "feel."

The exercise is important not because it's fun, but because it makes what you want clear. It is no different in the financial context than any other and in fact, money is often not the final point. A great vision is more likely to be a specific possession than a sum of currency. After all, what good is money by itself?

Visions are what you would like to see or experience in the future.

To complete an effective visioning, you need two things: a way to document your ideas, and enough time to do it.

I find many people have "mini" visionary processes through-out their life. They are helpful, but not sufficient for identifying what is *most* important. They can often be affected by emotions in the moment and other variables.

Great visioning will happen when you put away your computer and your phone and turn off the television. You are not distracted by media of any form. You're alone or with your loved ones who will be part of your plan. You have a pen and paper, a whiteboard, or some other way to document things quickly and eliminate items if needed. Ideally, you have at least an hour and probably more. Not having any time restriction is ideal. Also, making sure you are well fed going in or having some food and drink readily available is helpful.

In the process, you will allow your mind to relax. You will write down anything that comes to mind. It's likely your initial list might take thirty minutes and fill up quite a bit of space. This is essentially a brain dump of all your "mini" visioning sessions you've had throughout your life. Nothing can be disallowed. Some examples are:

I see our family doing mission work in Mexico (or wherever you prefer) three times per year with Habitat for Humanity.
I will pay off all my credit card debt.
I see us traveling with our family to our favorite vacation spot in Europe for our twenty-fifth anniversary.
I will open a consulting firm for construction companies.
I am going to retire from my corporate career and open an Italian restaurant.
I will build an emergency fund that would last six months.

I will write a book about personal finance and share the message with as many people as possible (I know the feeling!).

I am going to clear $100 in my budget to save for later.

I will buy a country home for my parents in Kansas (wherever their favorite place is).

We will fix the roof on our home.

Our family will found a non-profit organization to benefit victims of domestic violence.

We will purchase a new car with cash.

We will move to Norway and breed Siberian Husky sled dogs.

I will pay off my student loan.

I will travel the juggling circuit and start an Instagram page.

I will sell our furniture in storage, use the proceeds to put a down payment on a home, and pay the mortgage with the money I was using for the storage cost.

I will start a bilingual improv comedy club in our town.

I will meet with a financial planner and make decisions on our insurance and estate planning.

I am going to go back to school for my Master in Business Administration.

Notice the specificity. Nothing is wrong, but everything is detailed.

You might come up with some incredibly outlandish visions. Document them. They may not be so crazy in the future. What is most important is you identify what the top things are. You can't have fifteen most important things. It has to be five for less. Your brain and body won't be able to handle more concentrations. Visions will get blurry. You will burn out your motivation and limit your progress on all the items. It would be better to make faster progress on fewer items and as you complete some, you can add others. The good news is that you've documented all of them! They'll never go away unless you want them to.

After you and your loved ones have listed anything you possibly can (you might have 100), it's time for a break. A break might be a week long. I've found the need to reset the conversation at this point. The most recent items tend to skew your ideas and your brain is overloaded.

Once you've taken time away, get back to the same place and situation you were when starting your visioning. The next part of the process is narrowing down the list. This should be much faster. Usually, the first round of "cuts" is pretty easy. There will be some things that "pop" and you'll laugh that they even made it on the list (you'll probably eliminate them forever). All the rest make the first "cut."

Next, try to separate the things that seem to make the most sense. This might be about twenty items. All are likely to be addressed at some point. The rest can be saved to consider at a later date. Your final twenty now need to be divided. This is the hardest part. You have to pick your top five or less. There are two things to consider when doing this:

Which items are absolutely essential to life in the near-term future?

and

Which items will provide a foundation for my (or our) personal financial situation moving forward?

These two questions will often highlight at least a few things that can be chosen as your first concentrations. If you have room in your top five still, break down the remaining things by what you would like to see first and what is most possible.

Once you have your top list, you have completed visioning. It's time to celebrate! This must be acknowledged as a great accomplishment. You are much more likely to get to something when you know what it is. It may seem obvious, but the lack of an endpoint is what leads to people going financially astray. You'll now have the vision of what is most important and be much more likely to apply your actions to it.

Completing the visioning process leads directly into goal setting, but it is not the same.

Those who are able to turn their visions into goals are much more likely to have actionable steps that they desire to do. It's one thing to have a vision, it's another to have long-term goals, but it's best to have immediately actionable steps.

Create your goals with your vision as the guide. For example:

If your vision is to have a new car, your goal should be to save the amount of money needed to buy it.

Financial goal setting can be very similar to other forms of goal setting, but it has its own unique characteristics (unlike visioning). What makes financial goal setting different is money is very unpredictable. Investment returns are not guaranteed, income is often not guaranteed, the value of a currency is not guaranteed, and the currency (as mentioned in Chapter 3) is not guaranteed either. It is vital that goals can be monitored, and flexibility is important.

One popular goal-setting technique is using SMART goals.

Specific
Measurable
Achievable
Relevant
Time-Bound

I have used these criteria in the planning of various things in my life. They often apply well to the world. My business partner and I used them to create goals for our business, Initiate Impact. Our most important goal for 2021 was to partner with fifteen purpose-driven families to manage their financial life and steward their possessions for positive impact in the world.

This goal is specific because we identify exactly who we want to partner with and what we will do. Finer details are also documented.

It's measurable because we provide a number (fifteen). We will easily know if we hit the goal or not.

It's achievable based on our industry experience and expectations. We plan to do big things, but they have to be reasonable.

It's relevant because it aligns with the mission of our organization. We want to help families make the world a better place in the way they are uniquely qualified to.

It's time-bound because it is a goal for 2021. We have that period to reach it.

The vision for our company is much different than that of Jobs' for Apple, but the proper vision and goals are still necessary to define success for Initiate Impact.

These characteristics are a great way to help with the success of reaching your personal goals. In the financial sense, the measuring of the goals is of utmost importance. What good are the most well-calculated and tracked (using the tools referenced in Chapter 5) if there is no reference point for success?

Measuring your goals must be done but it can be deceiving, especially if your goal is long-term in nature. You must be aware of your vision as you make progress toward your goal. For example, if your vision is to retire at age seventy in Arizona with a fully owned home and the means to travel anywhere in the country to visit your grandkids, you have a great idea of what you want to be doing in the future. You might crunch some numbers and come up with a financial need of $500,000 to buy a home at that point and a need for $100,000 of income per year.

If you're forty years old at the time of the goal setting, you have thirty years until the age your vision shows for retirement. You really don't know how much that house is going to cost or what the cost of living will be in Arizona at that point. As time passes you will need to monitor your goal and adjust to stay locked with your vision.

You will need to set at least one goal related to each of your primary visionary points, but it is likely you will need a few. Sticking with the retirement in Arizona example, you'll need to save a certain amount of money, but it will be in different forms. You may have a savings goal in your 401(k) plan (the popular type of retirement savings vehicle mentioned in Chapter 12) provided by your employer, but that may not be a great place to come up with the money you need to pay for your house. You could set a savings goal there to cover your income in the future and plan on paying off an existing mortgage and selling that home to generate cash for the Arizona home.

HABITS FOR SUCCESS

You'll be excited to start executing your actionable steps once you have all of your goals and they are clearly tied to your visions. At that point, you'll want to develop great habits that will keep you on track.

Good habits are tied directly to the budgeting concepts in Chapter 4. Expenses that relate to your goals and visions are non-discretionary. You'll always want to consider this prior to making purchases. Make sure you are not influenced beyond your discretionary means by what you experience.

It's great that modern finance provides us with the tools to calculate just about anything in seconds. You can be pretty aggressive with your projections or you can take a conservative approach to give yourself more room for error. There are also numerous places to get information and inspiration. Each has its own level of intensity.

I spoke with Mark Glicini, a professional lacrosse player and mental performance coach. He trains people to achieve more of what they desire through specific mind development practices. In our conversation, we talked about the commonalities of people who are successful in reaching their goals whether physical, mental, or financial. He said, "consistency plus continuity equals results." This means those who develop strong habits and execute them over long periods of time eventually reach their goals.

I mentioned in Chapter 7 how speculation is a risky practice related to investments and not likely to end up well. Speculating about your goals is not advised either. You need to execute your personal financial plan consistently and with continuity across all aspects to have the best chance at reaching your goals. Each piece makes up part of the plan and if one is overlooked or treated with haste, it can be a detriment to the whole thing.

FINANCIAL INDEPENDENCE RETIRE EARLY

One strong movement in recent years that illustrated Mark's principles is called F.I.R.E. (Financial Independence Retire Early). Most would say they seek financial independence, but its definition can vary. In 1992, Vicki Robin and Joe Dominguez wrote *Your Money or Your Life*. This book concentrated on financial independence and provided great insight on how to reach it as soon as possible. It has since been updated to provide more timely information. The main premise is to find and have "enough" (and then some) rather than always seeking "more" and there is a nine-step process designed to transform your relationship with money.

F.I.R.E. became popular among younger professionals in the 2010s. It generally requires a fairly high income to execute, but regardless of how much money you make, it includes some great concepts and relies on consistency and continuity. It teaches living as minimalistic as possible to save as much of your income (in some cases as much as 70 percent) as you can when you are young.

In theory, F.I.R.E. will enable you to save enough to retire in your thirties or forties and do whatever you want the rest of your life. This takes tremendous discipline and is not for everyone. It has taken on some less stringent versions over the years and receives criticism for being unrealistic. The variations are:

Barista—a play on having a part-time job at a coffee place to supplement income in early retirement

Coast—you don't need the part-time job, but you need something to do

Lean—the most stringent approach maximizing savings and likely shortening the time to retirement as much as possible

Fat—a much less stringent approach allowing more free-spending and likely taking more time to achieve retirement

F.I.R.E. receives pushback because, just like any other concept, it doesn't work for everyone. Even when it does work, it has to be applied in a specific way that makes sense for an individual. Despite mixed opinions, there are certain key points we can take from the process:

- Visions are clear ideas of what we want in the future and are not necessarily financial.
- Goals are the things we need to do to make our visions a reality.
- Financial goals have an added importance of measurement and flexibility over other goals.
- Nothing beats a tight budget.
- Everyone's plan is unique to them.

Regardless of what strategy you use, solid budgeting is essential every time. Clear visions and goals will help you build your perfect financial pyramid. They are a critical component of any great plan—your bread and butter.

16.

A Penny Saved Is a Penny Earned

HOW TO HELP YOUR KIDS AND WHO TO ASK FOR HELP
I'm sure I wasn't the only kid to have a piggy bank. In fact, I know that as much as technology has taken over banking, piggy banks still exist today.

In my previous professional role, my team and I would often pass out piggy banks, and guess what color they were?

Blue!

There's something about the bright color that sticks out. Kids would come up to me and talk about their piggy banks and the "share," "save," and "spend" slots. These piggies were great because they taught more than just saving. They really helped young people understand budgeting and the different purposes for money.

It's important to teach indelible lessons to kids (like the lesson my piggy taught me). They need memories that can guide them to sound decision-making as they get older (and help them write a book). The best way to make something memorable is to offer it through experience.

Experiential learning gives young people a chance to form their own opinions and make their own decisions. It not only tests their intellect, but it trains emotional intelligence and allows for acceptable stress.

Stress gets a bad rap in society. Yet, it's actually stress that provides the opportunity for growth. The best way to train the body for something is to put it under pressure. Marathon runners don't make it 26.2 miles in a couple of hours without extreme training. They have to run consistently for years to reach their full potential. Even amateur runners use five-month training plans in which they are recommended to run up to five days a week. They must put the body through a lot to reach their goals. As I write this, my wife is training for the New York City Marathon. She's been training for months. It's been a lot of physical stress, but the benefits are amazing.

The rewarding sounds of coins dropping into the piggy bank were a different type of feedback than that of a marathon runner but a great way for me to experience saving money as a kid. There were times I experienced the feeling of being short of the amount of money I needed to buy what I wanted. I had to understand it takes time and consistency to reach a goal. That stress taught me how to persevere.

LET'S TALK ABOUT IT

Money should be talked about at the family dinner table. Concepts should be taught in school and kids shouldn't feel money the first time when they get some for their twelfth birthday. Teenagers need to know what they are getting themselves into when they apply for a student loan. When a twenty-two-year-old graduates from college, they must feel confident in budgeting their early adult life. The stress of finances should not be overwhelming.

Unfortunately, understanding the four mathematical operations (addition, subtraction, multiplication, and division) is not sufficient for personal financial management. They help you calculate your money but don't explain the concepts needed to allocate it (like sharing, saving, and spending from the piggy banks we handed out) and make wise financial decisions. More advanced statistics and algebra classes take students further down the educational path but still don't address the foundational concepts. The psychological and emotional side of finances must be experienced.

Kids need to be shown the value of money and be taught to control emotions when making decisions. They also need to understand it doesn't "grow on trees." It's great to provide for your children, but it's even greater to show them what it means to provide.

A child can be shown the value of money by experiencing limitations. They need to understand what it's like to not have the ability to acquire something. In addition, they should be taught how to earn. Not everyone is a lifelong entrepreneur, but they should be shown to work for something if they want it. Even the smallest lessons about effort will lead to future success.

TEACHING FINANCIAL LITERACY

Investopedia says financial literacy is the ability to understand and effectively use various financial skills, including personal financial management, budgeting, and investing.

Mint.com published a survey in 2020 with an eye-popping statistic. About 55 percent of adults are financially literate in the United States, Canada, France, Germany, Italy, Japan, and the United Kingdom. This means nearly half of adults are financially illiterate. Similar to a language, financial literacy can be taught to an adult, but it's harder for them to learn at that point.

We need to teach people the basics of finance before mental maturity. As they grow, they will develop great habits. They should be able to understand making money, how to spend it wisely, and how to save for the future. They also need to know the basics of investing, borrowing, how interest affects each of those, and how to protect for what they have worked hard. Some example activities to help young people learn about money are:

Earning—The good ol' fashioned lemonade stand—You can shop for lemons (or lemonade mix) with kids and keep track of the cost. Then they can sell lemonade and learn what it's like to earn an income.

Sharing—Have kids identify items (such as toys or clothes that are still in good condition) that they don't use much or would be willing to give up. Brainstorm with them who would put the items to better use and have them give the items away.

Saving—Plant some seeds. Have the kids tend to the plants that grow from the seeds. Explain how their savings needs to be tended to and "fed" just like a plant for it to grow.

Spending—Create a "mini" store of goods in the home that the kids normally use. Give the kids pretend money that adds up to enough money for most but not all of the goods. Allow them to spend the pretend money and decide how to allocate what they've budgeted.

Mint published two other statistics that are strikingly related.

One in four parents reported they never or almost never talk to their kids about household finances and *as of July 2019, 28 percent of US adults had no emergency savings.* There is no proof of a correlation between the two of these, but if 25 percent of kids don't hear about money at home, it seems to me that might be a subset of the 28 percent of adults who don't have an emergency fund.

Those who don't have an emergency fund are putting themselves at risk, but if they don't understand the importance of the fund, they are not likely to maintain one. They may not recognize the risk because they are not used to identifying it. Better understanding is all they need. Children who have been taught the basics of personal finance from a young age are more likely to apply the principles to their adult lives and budgets when they need to.

"NUMBER MUNCHERS" STILL HOLDS UP

When I was growing up, I learned about numbers by playing "Number Munchers" on the Apple computers my elementary school had. Steve Jobs' vision was manifest in that school and technology seemed to be helpful. These days, there are so many technological sources to take the attention of children. In addition to distracting, our tablets and phones also make things seem overly accessible. Young people can jump between programs with ease and it generates the expectations of immediate satisfaction.

There is proof in how deep the relationships people can develop with the technology they engage. In her book *Alone Together*, Sherry Turkle examines numerous examples. She studied robotic pets like the Tamagotchi, Furby, and aibo. There were mixed results and different lessons from all the studies, but the evidence overwhelmingly showed kids developed relationships with these toys. Even in short periods of time, they learned to interact with the technology that today would be considered relatively primitive. Today's toys and devices are more advanced. Kids can have multiple robotic pets in one device or application.

Children will interact with and learn from whatever is available. Therefore, modern technology will never be "ahead" of them. They will be right with it, gathering information. We must ensure what they pick up will be helpful. Turkle says, "Because we have grown up with the net, we think the net is grown up." Young people just assume the internet is the place to get information. Turkle also says, "Every new technology challenges us generation after generation to ask whether it serves our human purposes."

If we help young people experience financial literacy through today's social channels, they will grow into wise financial decision-makers. They will apply the principles to their lives and modern media and technology will not lead them astray no matter how many offers they receive and options they have every day. In fact, they will use the technology to their advantage.

It's up to parents to teach their children by providing a good example. You don't have to make a lot of money or have a special title to do this well. In fact, the tighter your budget, the more you can illustrate the importance of great money habits. Living paycheck to paycheck is not bad. It's living beyond your means that causes the problem.

THE PROVIDER AND THE GREATEST TEACHER
Providing for your family is one of the noblest things you can do. It's hard, but a natural inclination. It takes planning but must be as flexible as possible and will ultimately be the greatest lesson you can provide. You can think of it as a well-executed business, but it can also be like a wild train ride. This is where you are the greatest teacher. You never know what kind of expenses can arise. Kids have accidents, things happen in your home, and illnesses can arise. Not every expense is a catastrophe and the case of numerous

smaller items can cause a roller-coaster effect. In all cases though, you must make it work.

You will teach your family while also providing for them. When you give your children vegetables, you tell them they need to eat them because they're healthy. When you help them with their homework, you tell them it's important because they should get good grades. The same applies to money.

One well-known habit for parents to put money in the hands of their kids is allowance. This is a good technique for teaching earnings and savings (as long as they are not encouraged to spend right away).

Another lesser-used technique is to take money away from your kids. I suppose you could fine them for making mistakes like bad language or attitude, but I'm referring to something else.

For a modern technology application, you can use some of the services mentioned in Chapter 6 as a guide to illustrate how giving an allowance or taking money away affects what they have.

When my father was a young adult and moved back in with his parents, they allowed it on one condition. He had to pay rent. You might think this is a harsh request for a broke college kid, but in actuality it was brilliant.

Dad had to pay his parents every month while he was living with them. He wasn't allowed to freeload. After a year of living back at home, he was ready to move to his own place. On the day he moved out, his dad (my grandfather) handed him a check for the value of all the "rent" he paid. This was a powerful exchange. A father gave his son two things: a check for thousands of dollars and a great lesson in savings (and maybe some entrepreneurship).

My grandfather provided for his son financially when he was a minor but provided a great lesson when he was a young adult. I would love to have experienced the moment when he gave the money back and what was said. It could have been a simple passing of an envelope, or it could have been a formal celebration. Either way, it was a great teaching moment.

It's just as important to teach things to those you love as it is to give things to them. As in the above example, experiential learning is preferred. "Acting" paycheck to paycheck is a great way for a household to experience the basics of financial literacy.

THE MONETARY TOOL

A paycheck is more than a sum of money. It's a tool. It not only pays bills, but it teaches lessons. No matter how much money you make, or how much you spend, every paycheck should be considered. Your budget may be in order and you're not in danger of missing any payments, but you should still address your income.

Do you remember zero-based budgeting from Chapter 5? The concept was popularized by Peter Pyrrh in his book *Zero Based Budgeting: A Practical Management Tool for Evaluating*

Expenses. Pyrrh was an accounting manager for Texas Instruments. He used the process for allocating the expenses of his large employer and making sure every dollar had a purpose. He once called zero-based budgeting a "tremendous" tool and in relation to the business world noted, "especially in times of economic problems, when you need to make reductions, or when you have significant and rapid technological change." It's a good tool in relation to advancing technology and if a big company with a much more complex situation than a single family can use the process effectively, it's appropriate for any household.

A zero-based budget is a great way to slow down the wild train that is providing for your family and also teach young people to assign a purpose to each dollar they have. The goal is not to "spend" every dollar, but none should go undirected. Savings, along with paying your bills, is one of the important line items. You have to pay yourself. The budget reaches zero every time and if for some reason you don't spend some of the money you expected to, you can save some extra that month.

Financial management is not a static process. Life changes and so does a budget along with it. It's not about developing the perfect plan and letting it run. It's somewhat of a nurturing process, especially when there is change. You have to consider new scenarios and see how they go.

Suppose you move to a new home in a new area. You will have to wait a few months before you get a feel for what your utility bill will be. What's the cost of water and power? What unexpected expenses will arise? You must monitor these items and keep track of them (thankfully, technology makes it easy). Then, adjust your budget.

SHOULD YOU SEEK PROFESSIONAL ASSISTANCE?

You may come to a point where comprehensive professional assistance is needed. The point is different for everyone and is separate from isolated services such as tax preparation or drafting of legal documents as those discussed in Chapter 13. It is important to consider these three questions when determining if you need professional financial assistance:

1. Do you understand all of the aspects of your and your family's financial life?
2. Do you feel you have the time to handle everything or vet professionals that do?
3. Do you desire to take on these tasks or would you prefer to do other things?

If the answer to any of those is "no," you should consider searching for a provider of professional financial services. There are different types of experts in the industry and what they specialize in is more important than their title. Some title examples are financial advisor, financial professional, financial planner, and wealth manager. One way to educate yourself beyond a title is to look at what service providers have spent years of professional education time on. The Financial Industry Regulatory Authority (FINRA) provides a list of designations that financial professionals can hold. Three of the most prominent are:

- CFA®—Chartered Financial Analyst, These are professionals with expertise in investment analysis and portfolio management.
- CFP®—Certified Financial Planner, These are professionals who take a holistic, personalized approach to bring all the pieces of your financial life together.
- CPA—Certified Public Accountant, These are professionals with expertise in accounting and tax preparation that help individuals, families, businesses, and other organizations reach their financial goals.

There is no catch-all designation, but I would recommend asking anyone who you are considering hiring these seven questions:

1. What is your expertise?
2. How much experience do you have serving in that specific area?
3. What are the types of individuals and families that you best serve?
4. How are you compensated and what do your services cost?
5. What does your service model look like and how long is a typical engagement?
6. What is the time commitment from each of us?
7. How do you determine if it is in our best interest to work together?

With an answer to these questions, you'll be able to get a feel if the person can help you. If they are a trustworthy person, they should tell you if they believe they can be of assistance or not. Ultimately, it's your decision, and more important than anything is if you feel a rapport with the person and their team.

Make sure you feel comfortable with a potential financial professional and that they show genuine desire for your well-being. Kevin Keller, the chief executive officer of the CFP® Board, described to me a modern financial planning process as "digitally enabled but human delivered because there is so much emotion." However, you should not be intimidated. It was reassuring that Keller also said, "The good thing is there are a number of reputable, financial service firms that are making product or advice offerings available for people."

COMBINING HUMAN ADVICE WITH MODERN TECHNOLOGY

In addition to the technical expertise I mentioned, a great advisor should also be able to relieve the emotional stresses that Keller mentioned and use technology to assist you in your financial matters. I also spoke with Jason Wenk, the founder and CEO of Altruist. He describes the company as a technology firm. They act as a financial custodian—a financial institution that holds customers' securities for safekeeping to prevent them from being stolen or lost. They describe themselves as an all-in-one platform that helps your financial advisor give you a delightful experience with your money and are on a mission to make financial advice better and more accessible to everyone.

I asked Wenk about how technology is affecting the industry. In reference to the consumers who are using new-age investment applications, he said, "They're being fooled in many cases by really clever marketing, branding, graphics, and gamification into doing things that benefit the app developer, the venture investors, and private equity firms. They cost, at times, a lot more than they help the consumer."

Clever marketing is selling the excitement of speculating and modern technology is allowing access. The access is great but not the excitement. As mentioned in Chapters 11 and 13, some parts of our financial lives just aren't exciting. This certainly doesn't minimize their importance though. In actuality, a lot of personal finance is boring. If you try to make it exciting, it might end up like that in a way you regret.

A great advisor knows how to use the available technologies to make things simple and consistent. This does sound boring which is why hiring someone to do it might be prudent. I feel there is a need to connect professionals and consumers around this topic while making it more enjoyable. Altruist has a noble mission. Maybe if professionals can serve more people because of great technology, money will be less stressful, less avoided in the home, and a more well-understood topic.

Whether you are prepared to hire a professional or still at a stage where you believe you are your own best advisor, I must stress the importance of having a personal or family-specific plan.

Wenk also said, "The idea of the influencer economy has sort of trickled its way into financial influence." There is no way an influencer can understand what your individual situation is, even if they are of good intent. This is not to discredit every person trying to share good ideas about money on the internet. However, you have to consider everything a piece of information and not personalized advice.

The influencer who tempts you to buy a fancy car is definitely not an advisor. The YouTube channel about investing may actually share accurate information, but it's a lot harder to determine if it's valuable or just tempting you with excitement.

There should be a personal finance YouTube channel that is perfectly boring. Would you want to watch that? Me either. In my conversation with Wenk, he provided an example of an undesirable consumer experience with advisory technology where the professional believed their technology to be state of the art. The person failed to realize the user experience was cumbersome. The technology stack was powerful, but there were too many places to log into and too many passwords and usernames to remember.

The experience on an application like Robinhood, which was mentioned in Chapter 7, is much different than the one above. It's enjoyable. There is competition for investors. Hopefully, firms like Altruist will be able to combine technology and the simple, consistent advice that many of us need.

AUTOMATED, BUT FLEXIBLE

A flexible plan allows you to make changes as needed but is not hasty. It provides guidelines for basic situations and has a general purpose so when something unexpected happens, there is some direction. It is prepared to pivot and avoid disaster.

Technology, when effective, is engaging but will allow you to automate and accurately predict expenditures and inflows. If it's engaging, it can teach you and your family about great financial habits around topics like sharing, saving, and spending. If it automates the traditional aspects of budgeting, you'll spend more time thinking about the major lifestyle decisions that can get a little overwhelming, especially if decision fatigue would otherwise set in.

There is no "perfect" budget, but there is a perfect budget for you and your family. There is a great way for you to provide *for* your loved ones and give indelible lessons *to* them.

Every paycheck matters. Every dollar matters. Every lesson matters.

A penny saved is a penny earned and a lesson learned.

17.

You Can't Buy Happiness

WHAT MATTERS MOST

One of my good friends has three children. They are all good kids, but one of them the family calls "easy." They never have to worry about the "easy" child. This kid will always stay out of danger, make good decisions, and represent the family well. Honestly, I feel the presence of some more experienced or relaxed parenting. The parents are just a bit more confident because they've raised other kids. There is a lot less stress because there isn't much they haven't seen. It's almost as if many of their parenting decisions are automated effectively, recharacterizing these decisions as given steps in a process rather than decisions.

The best thing this text could provide you is unwavering confidence in your ability to evaluate financial decisions. It will do that by helping you create a blueprint and by making technology a tool that helps you manage your personal financial life and eliminate many of the stressful decisions you have to make. A healthy relationship with the tool and, as a result, a great money mindset will lead to a positive financial life experience.

HEALTHY RELATIONSHIPS

Princeton University's Woodrow Wilson School did a study in 2010 that showed an income of $75,000 was the limit at which money could "buy happiness." In other words, anything above that amount would not make you happier. In 2021, University of Pennsylvania's The Wharton School published a study that indicated differently. Ironically, an app was used to track people's happiness throughout the day. They answered questions using the app to document how they felt. Technology had its say.

Matthew Killingsworth, a senior fellow at Penn's Wharton School, led the study which found income above $75,000 did lead to greater happiness. Killingsworth believes people who have more money have more options. Things are more flexible. The COVID-19 pandemic illustrated this point well as people who had more of a cushion were less affected by job losses and salary cuts. However, Killingsworth also said, "Although money might be good for happiness, I found people who equated money and success were less happy than those who didn't. I also found people who earned more money worked longer hours and felt more pressed for time."

Money can give you more control, but it alone will not buy you happiness. I believe it brings opportunities, good and bad. It's stressful when you can't pay your bills. The solution everyone wishes they had was to make more. Unfortunately,

Mo Money Mo Problems, the posthumously released song by The Notorious B.I.G., was prophetic. Or, maybe it wasn't that prophetic. Maybe it was just a fact of the day and for all time. The more money you have, the more you can spend, but the more responsibility you have.

Another study that started in 1938 points to relationships being the greatest sign of happiness. Amazingly, the study is still going on to this day. It has spanned across generations. It began during the Great Depression with a group of sophomores at Harvard University (including future president John F. Kennedy) and lasted beyond the tragic passing of Biggie Smalls in 1997. But somehow the famed rapper had some related wisdom.

The study's original group of subjects totaled 268. One thousand three hundred of the subject's children were added and control groups have since been expanded further. The *Harvard Gazette* reported on April 11, 2017, nineteen of the original cohort were still alive. The study is now over eighty years old and much data has pointed to the fact that relationships have an incredibly strong effect on people's health and longevity.

Every two years, subjects and their families are asked about mental and emotional wellness. Medical records and blood samples are examined. Scientists wanted to understand how life's situations and events affect the subjects physically, mentally, and emotionally.

Over the years it has been proven the subjects with the highest quality relationships had the healthiest lives regardless of successes and failures as measured by money or societal expectations. Robert Waldinger, director of the Harvard Study of Adult Development, said, "The clearest message we get from this seventy-five-year study is this: Good relationships keep us happier and healthier. Period."

LIMITING STRESS

The average person avoids great stress by being able to cover their expenses. This means an adjustment in expenses could also be just as helpful as an increase in income. If you've covered the essentials, don't create more stress by taking on additional consistent expenditures, limit unwarranted isolated spending, and use technology to keep track of your budget (zero-based, of course).

Maybe just balancing your budget isn't good enough. It seems we also need to balance our emotions and relationships. The great news about this is a healthy relationship with technology can simultaneously help us with our budget and allow us more time to spend building and maintaining quality interpersonal relationships.

Sherry Turkle also wrote in *Alone Together*, "To combat addiction you have to discard the addicting substance. But, we are not going to get rid of the internet. We will not go cold turkey or forbid cell phones to our children." We have acknowledged the addictive problems that internet technology poses. Yet, we are not going to shut it down because its benefits can outweigh the drawbacks. Turkle suggests, "We have to find a way to live with seductive technology and make it work to our purposes." I believe it is vital to identify the key purposes for you. If we are not going to eliminate it, then each person's time spent should be for their own good reasons.

Identifying what is most interesting to you makes it much easier to isolate the things you should spend your resources on and limit our spending to just those things. Robert Greene provides a foundational suggestion in his book, *The Laws of Human Nature*, when he says, "Instead of constantly chasing after the latest trends and modeling our desires on what others find exciting, we should spend our time getting to know our own tastes and desires better so that we can distinguish what is something that we truly need or want from that which has been manufactured by advertisers or viral effects." This statement is somewhat freeing. It allows us to make our own decisions as to what is important.

We can take control of our desires. Our minds should experience the agility and efficiency of technology while applying the wisdom needed for sound decision-making. Later in his text, Greene defines the ideal state of mind as "one that retains the flexibility of youth along with the reasoning powers of an adult." In some ways, the internet keeps us all youthful. It's up to us to apply the reasoning powers.

If we can identify the things most important to us, we can set a baseline of rules for decision-making. This essentially removes the need for another decision. It has already been made. We can avoid decision fatigue and those challenging choices can become positive habits, similar to the experienced parent who isn't overwhelmed when raising their youngest child. Once you have good habits, their effects compound.

You begin to experience consistent positive feedback and your brain is in a better position to make the real, challenging decisions, like the major financial type.

Your goal should be to reach James Clear's plateau of latent potential, referenced in Chapter 1. There is great news that you now have some great ideas that can help form the cues, cravings, responses, and rewards of some positive feedback loops. The plateau is the point at which you realize the progress you've made related to a consistent effort. You've had the ability the whole time, but you had to reach a certain level of proficiency for your efforts to be apparent.

A good example of latent potential can be taken from the examples in Chapter 10 of paying off loans. It could be overwhelming thinking about owing a lot to many different lenders. If you can pay off just one card, you'd probably feel like you've arrived atop the plateau of latent potential when closing the account and seeing the progress. You'd see your ultimate goal in reach.

To reach the plateau, you need to create a great habit loop. The cue is your monthly bill triggering your brain that it's time to pay something. It's obvious. You're reminded you have an opportunity to make it one step closer to your goal. It's an attractive positive craving. You now have to respond. You make the response easy by linking your bank account to your credit card company's mobile application. You could even set it on autopay because you know the exact amount you intend to pay (you may want to manually pay it as part of the exercise). Finally, the reward provides satisfaction. Watching the amount you owe go down could be enough. You may also want to consider awarding yourself a special dinner or something else enjoyable after each debt is paid in full.

MY NEWFOUND (EFFECTIVE) SLEEP SCHEDULE

I used to be a night person. I think it was because I had trouble sleeping by myself growing up as an only child. Sadly, my blue piggy bank couldn't solve this problem. I would lay awake until the early morning well into adulthood. I used to feel sorry for myself and blamed it on nature. However, I learned a big lesson during the COVID-19 pandemic.

My wife and I enjoy exercising together. For over a decade, it was usually something we did on weeknights. The far majority of those workouts were after long days at work when it was dark and we were hungry. We enjoyed each other's company, but not the exercise. I have always believed exercise is far less effective for you physically when it's not enjoyable. What I didn't realize is there can be many other benefits. We would come home from the gym, eating, and bed (not sleep, for me) didn't come long after that.

The coronavirus led to an incredibly grueling schedule for my wife and many other teachers and their schools. She wasn't getting home until seven o'clock in the evening, and by the time we were finished working out, it was almost ten o'clock. She had to get up at six a.m. This wasn't sustainable.

So, what did we do? We decided to get up even earlier. We started working out early in the morning. This took some discomfort and discipline. The alarm cued us to rise. We craved being done with the dreaded workout before the sun came up. We responded by doing it.

We thought the reward was simply not having to work out at night. However, we learned there were plenty of other benefits. We now crave the superior exercise performance, post-workout endorphins, improvements in our level of fitness, increased productivity, and the schedule is just a bonus.

Counterintuitively, I now fall asleep faster and sleep more soundly by getting up earlier. We have developed an amazingly satisfying habit loop. In addition, technology adds to this experience by helping us track our progress, learn about more techniques and methods for training, and ultimately add to the loop.

MORE MONEY AND MORE JOY

Positive financial habits supplemented by technology will have the same effect on your life as our new schedule did for me. The reasons for budgeting, saving, and investing wisely go way beyond your net worth. I couldn't begin to list all of the possible items, and each person's situation is unique, but the stresses that money causes are not to be minimized. According to CNBC, money and relationship stress in the home are related. Thirty-five percent of respondents in a SunTrust Bank study released in 2015 said money was the primary cause of stress in their partnership.

If money causes so many problems, it must get rid of a lot of them too, right? Unfortunately, we know money can provide opportunities, but it's ultimately not a problem solver. This tells us forming healthy habits is actually more effective than a windfall. Remember the *Washington Post* statistic from Chapter 3 (70 percent of people who receive a large windfall or win the lottery end up going broke)?

The Grant Study showed us healthy relationships are most important to our long-term wellness. This is not the experience of a lottery winner gone broke. They are likely to have lived it up upon winning. In the long run, though, they suffered. Let a positive relationship in your life be with money. Make it so you appreciate thinking about your finances even if it's related to debt or estate planning. This doesn't mean you can't have a good relationship with money if you win the lotto. It just means a large sum of money will not guarantee joy or health.

I have also found there is an emphasis on technology and relationships amongst professionals in the world of finance. John Loper, the managing director of professional practice for the CFP® Board shared with me that the board has received feedback from professionals they certify, which shows that "the growth of technology has actually stressed the importance of relationships." He also said, "information is abundant and free, but advice is scarce and costly." This reinforces the importance of finding the right people to consult for financial matters, as discussed in Chapter 16. This is a vital relationship and is worth the proper amount of time.

Remember to identify what you need and what you want (which is not money) as you begin and adjust your personal financial journey. With those in mind, you can use a lot of your 2,617 daily taps, swipes, and clicks to provide you with more valuable time, consume within your defined limits, and manage your personal finances wisely. You won't be just looking for "more," whether mindless distractions or money. Technology won't slow your progress or change how you think. Instead, it will supplement what you already know, make you more efficient, and assist in your efforts. Your valuable time will be expressed in positive relationships that are worth more than any sum of money. So, time is actually not money. It's better.

I believe we live in a very public world. We can connect with almost anyone, anytime, anywhere. This is one of the greatest things about the modern world. It also makes me excited for the innovations yet to come. I can't even imagine where we'll be in the future. I guarantee technologies will be much different. We might be on another planet. Cryptocurrency might rule our monetary system. Interest rates will be different. I doubt the real envelope system will be used in the future. Fifty-six thousand modems might be fossilized, and maybe Apple will still be making tools for the mind that advance humankind. Maybe we'll be insuring our hover crafts or teleportation machines instead of our cars and motorcycles, but one thing remains: *us*. We will share life with other people, and that is most important.

Socrates lived mostly in the fifth century BC, but his thoughts about personal relationships are timeless.

"There is no possession more valuable than a good and faithful friend."

It applied then and will hold up in another couple of millennia.

Whether the world of your day is public or private, it's what's personal that matters most.

Acknowledgments

———

I must acknowledge those who have given this book, and the information in it, the momentum it needed to grow into what it has become:

Nate Andorsky, Jess Bost, Sylvia Brown, Alex Gladstein, Jamie Hopkins, Alexis Jenkins, Kevin Keller, David Lenok, John Loper, Hannah Moore, Joe Nolan, Dr. Travis Parry, Dr. Wade Pfau, Tyrone Ross Jr., and Jason Wenk.

I'd also like to gratefully acknowledge the following people for supporting the book in its revision process:

Ryan Murdock, Josh Brandfon, Jennifer Batty, Rebecca Warren, Eric Koester, Jeremy and Kristin Becker, Beth Engerer, Jenn Sander, Gunnar and Darcy Esiason, Dave and Liz Kuhlman, Steve Isador, Carey and Jamie Halula, Erik Berns, Flora Yang, Simon Granner, Tiffany Mosher, Jamie and Joglie Quintanilla, Alaa, Khassa, Steve Mielke, Ed and Norma Sander, Chris Zimmerman, Anna Littlefield, Ben Arnold, Angel Aloma, Molly Rauschert, Jodi Carlson, Anjana Sreedhar, Nike Anani, Keith Mensendiek, Joe Nolan, Daniel and

Michaela Martinez, Jamie Bosse, Danny Cabrera, Brad Wales, Matt and Sydney Martin, Justin and Nora Brooks, Joseph Flagg Jr., Eric Villanueva, Bill Dwyer, John Lore, Don and Kristi Pitts, Dustin and Stacee Jacobs, Sean and Christina Yerkes, Mike and Debbie Sander, Roxanne Sander, Nora Miskolczi, Greg and Melissa Lovine, Wolf and Gabrielle Liebertz, Johannes Vergouwen, Mikey Vergouwen, Jamie Russo, Gigi DePasquale, John and Natalia Leavitt, John Lewis, Jim and Teri Lewis, and Phil Dicanzio.

Finally, but most importantly, to my loved ones who provided me the needed support and inspiration to write the text:

My father Bob, my mother Sue, my wife Trisha, my other parents, Gene and Beth Engerer, my sister-in-law, Jamie Halula, her husband, Carey, and their children: Lilly, Bennett, and Maia Halula.

Appendix

____

Introduction

CNBC. "Americans paid off a record $83 billion in credit card debt in 2020." March 8, 2021. https://www.cnbc.com/2021/03/08/americans-paid-off-a-record-83-billion-in-credit-card-debt-in-2020.html.

Federal Reserve Bank of New York. "Total Household Debt Climbs in Q2 2021, New Extensions of Credit Hit Series Highs." August 3, 2021. https://www.newyorkfed.org/newsevents/news/research/2021/20210803.

Greene, Tim. "More Than Just a Modem Man." March 8, 2004. https://www.networkworld.com/article/2331175/more-than-just-a-modem-man.html.

Lemelson-MIT "Brent Townshend. 56k Bit/sec Modem." Accessed October 6, 2021. https://lemelson.mit.edu/resources/brent-townshend.

Market Watch. "US credit card debt rises as COVID-related stimulus payments level off." Last updated August 4, 2021. https://www.marketwatch.com/story/credit-card-debt-increased-by-17-billion-in-2q-as-stimulus-payments-level-off-11628006712.

Naftulin, Julia. "Here's how many times we touch our phones every day." Business Insider. July 13, 2016. https://www.businessinsider.com/dscout-research-people-touch-cell-phones-2617-times-a-day-2016-7.

Nelson, Patrick. "We touch our phones 2,617 times a day, says study." Networkworld, Disruptor. July 7, 2016. https://www.networkworld.com/article/3092446/we-touch-our-phones-2617-times-a-day-says-study.html.

Northwestern Mutual. "Planning and Progress Study 2019." May 17th, 2019 https://news.northwesternmutual.com/planning-and-progress-2019.

Winnick, Michael. "Putting a Finger on Our Phone Obsession, Mobile touches: a study on how humans use technology." dscout. June 16, 2016. https://blog.dscout.com/mobile-touches.

Chapter 1

Clear, James. "Atomic Habits." Read by the author. Penguin Publishing Group, Published October 16, 2018. Chapter 1 13:35. Audible audio ed. 5 hr., 35 min.

Cristol, Hope. "What is Dopamine?" WebMD. Accessed October 6, 2021. https://www.webmd.com/mental-health/what-is-dopamine.

Giblin, Chris. "10 Most Interesting, Superstitious Rituals of Professional Athletes." Men's Journal, accessed October 6, 2001. https://www.mensjournal.com/sports/10-most-interesting-superstitious-rituals-of-professional-athletes/.

JD. "The Best Zig Ziglar Quotes that Will Inspire Your Success." Sources of Insight, accessed October 6, 2021. https://sourcesofinsight.com/zig-ziglar-quotes/

Lembke, Anna. "Digital Addictions Are Drowning Us in Dopamine." Wall Street Journal, August 13, 2021. https://www.wsj.com/articles/digital-addictions-are-drowning-us-in-dopamine-11628861572?mod=e2fb&fbclid=IwAR22-jzgkmAJsY-88ePmg8K_Lw9RJ10N4kwFemzPXiMq99i-GlHkgErZ9gTc.

Mandal, Ananya, MD. "Dopamine Functions." Last Updated April 9, 2019. News Medical. https://www.news-medical.net/health/Dopamine-Functions.aspx

NPR. "Brain Maturity Extends Well Beyond Teen Years." October 10, 2011. https://www.npr.org/templates/story/story.php?storyId=141164708.

Paradigm Treatment. "A Teen's Brain Isn't Fully Developed Until Age 25." February 23, 2021. https://paradigmtreatment.com/teens-brain-fully-developed-age/.

Chapter 2

Alter, Adam. "Irresistible." Read by the Author. Penguin Publishing Group, published March 6, 2018. Prologue 3:15, 3:55, 4:33, 5:54, 14:15. Audible audio ed. 8 hr., 17 min.

Alter, Adam. "Irresistible." Read by the Author. Penguin Publishing Group, published March 6, 2018. Chapter 2 32:56, 33:16. Audible audio ed. 8 hr., 17 min.

Clear, James. "Atomic Habits." Read by the author. Penguin Publishing Group, published October 16, 2018. Chapter 3. Audible audio ed. 5 hr., 35 min.

Szymkowski, Sean. "Americans are spending more time than ever behind the wheel." The Car Connection. Published March 1, 2019. https://www.thecarconnection.com/news/1121763_americans-are-spending-more-time-than-ever-behind-the-wheel.

Chapter 3

Housel, Morgan. "The Psychology of Money." Narrated by Chris Hil. Harriman House, Published September 8, 2020. Introduction 7:12, 12:00. Audible audio ed. 5 hr., 48 min.

Housel, Morgan. "The Psychology of Money." Narrated by Chris Hil. Harriman House, Published September 8, 2020. Chapter 4 7:03. Audible audio ed. 5 hr., 48 min.

Housel, Morgan. "The Psychology of Money." Narrated by Chris Hil. Harriman House, Published September 8, 2020. Chapter 9 2:42. Audible audio ed. 5 hr., 48 min.

Investopedia. "The Lottery; Is it Ever Worth Playing?" Accessed October 6, 2021. https://www.investopedia.com/managing-wealth/worth-playing-lottery/.

Lowenstein, George. "Five Myths About the Lottery." *The Washington Post,* December 27, 2019. https://www.washingtonpost.com/outlook/five-myths/five-myths-about-the-lottery/2019/12/27/742b9662-2664-11ea-ad73-2fd294520e97_story.html.

O'Connor, David. "Americans Spend Around $72B on Lottery Tickets Annually, Massachusetts Residents Play Most." Casino.org. Updated November 22, 2019. https://www.casino.org/news/americans-spent-nearly-72b-on-lottery-tickets-in-2017/.

Rand, Ayn. "Atlas Shrugged." Random House, 1957.

"The rise and fall of Madoff's Ponzi scheme." April 24, 2021. Reveal. Podcast, 11:30. https://revealnews.org/podcast/the-rise-and-fall-of-madoffs-ponzi-scheme/.

Chapter 4

Huddleston, Tom Jr. "Why retired NFL star Rob Gronkowski never spent a dime of his NFL salary." CNBC, Updated August 30, 2019. https://www.cnbc.com/2019/08/28/why-retired-nfl-star-rob-gronkowski-never-spent-his-nfl-salary.html.

Chapter 5

Amadeo, Kimberly. "Components of GDP Explained." The Balance, reviewed June 26, 2020. https://www.thebalance.com/components-of-gdp-explanation-formula-and-chart-3306015.

Amadeo, Kimberly. "Consumer Spending and its Impact on the Economy." The Balance, reviewed September 27, 2020. https://

www.thebalance.com/components-of-gdp-explanation-formula-and-chart-3306015.

Backman, Maurie. "You don't need that: Average American spends almost $18,000 a year on nonessentials." USA Today, May 7, 2019. https://www.usatoday.com/story/money/2019/05/07/americans-spend-thousands-on-nonessentials/39450207/.

Bureau of Economic Analysis. "Consumer Spending by State." 2019. https://www.bea.gov/data/gdp/gross-domestic-product.

Bureau of Economic Analysis. "Gross Domestic Product." 2nd Quarter 2021. https://www.bea.gov/data/gdp/gross-domestic-product.

Bureau of Labor Statistics. "Employee Tenure in 2020." US Department of Labor. News Release, September 22, 2020.

Casselman, Ben. "Surge in start-ups is a surprise in the pandemic economy." New York Times, February 17, 2021. https://www.nytimes.com/2021/02/17/business/pandemic-entrepreneurs.html.

Data Commons. "United States of America." 2020. https://datacommons.org/place/country/USA?utm_medium=explore&mprop=amount&popt=EconomicActivity&cpv=activitySource%2CGrossDomesticProduction&hl=en.

Discover. "The Beginner's Guide to Budgeting with the 50–20–30 Rule." Accessed October 6, 2021. https://www.discover.com/online-banking/banking-topics/budgeting-with-the-50-20-30-rule/.

Doyle, Allison. "Average Salary Information for US Workers." The Balance, Updated March 23, 2021. https://www.thebalancecareers.com/average-salary-information-for-us-workers-2060808.

Fernando, Jason. "Gross Domestic Product (GDP)." Investopedia. Updated September 8, 2021. https://www.investopedia.com/terms/g/gdp.asp.

Fiorillio, Steve. "The Average Income in the US" The Street, February 3, 2019. https://www.thestreet.com/personal-finance/average-income-in-us-14852178.

India.com. "In PICS: World's Largest Sandcastle in Denmark Makes it to Guinness World Records—Planning a Visit?" Published July 16, 2021. https://www.india.com/travel/articles/world-largest-sandcastle-denmark-guinness-world-records-see-photos-4818458/.

Investopedia. "Consumer Spending." August 11, 2021. https://www.investopedia.com/terms/c/consumer-spending.asp.

Simovic, Dragomir. "39 Entrepreneur Statistics You Need to Know in 2021." Small Biz Genius, August 19, 2021. https://www.smallbizgenius.net/by-the-numbers/entrepreneur-statistics/#gref.

Smith, Jen. "The 8 Best Budgeting Apps: Here's What We Loved and Hated." The Penny Hoarder, Updated April 27, 2021. https://www.thepennyhoarder.com/budgeting/best-budgeting-apps/?aff_sub2=homepage.

Trading Economics. "United States Consumer Spending." 2nd
Quarter 2020. Accessed October 6, 2021. https://tradingeco-
nomics.com/united-states/consumer-spending#:~:text=Con-
sumer%20Spending%20in%20the%20United%20States%20
averaged%206021.61%20USD%20Billion,the%20first%20quar-
ter%20of%201950.

Whiteside, Eric. "What Is the 50/20/30 Budget Rule?" Investopedia,
Reviewed on October 8, 2020. https://www.investopedia.com/
ask/answers/022916/what-502030-budget-rule.asp.

Chapter 6

Amadeo, Kimberly. "Economic Depression, Its Causes, and How to
Prevent It." The Balance, Reviewed May 23, 2021. https://www.
thebalance.com/what-is-an-economic-depression-3306013.

Federal Deposit Insurance Corporation. "2017 FDIC National Survey of Unbanked and Underbanked Households." Updated
October 19, 2020. https://www.fdic.gov/analysis/house-
hold-survey/2017/index.html.

Investopedia. "The Great Recession." Reviewed October 23, 2020.
https://www.investopedia.com/terms/g/great-recession.asp.

The Long View. September 8, 2021. 22:53. Podcast

Loudenback, Tanza. "How much you'll get in your next stimulus check, in simple charts." Business Insider. March 11, 2021.
https://www.businessinsider.com/personal-finance/how-
much-is-the-third-stimulus-check-2021-3.

National Commission on the Causes of the Financial and Economic Crisis in the United States. "The Financial Crisis Inquiry Report." February 25, 2011. https://www.govinfo.gov/content/pkg/GPO-FCIC/pdf/GPO-FCIC.pdf.

Segal, Troy. "What Was the Great Depression?" Investopedia. April 23, 2021. https://www.investopedia.com/terms/g/great_depression.asp.

Chapter 7

Curry, David. "Robinhood Revenue and Usage Statistics (2021)." Business of Apps. Updated October 5, 2021. https://www.businessofapps.com/data/robinhood-statistics/.

Financial Content. "GameStop Corp." Accessed October 6, 2021. https://markets.financialcontent.com/stocks/quote/historical?Symbol=321%3A2274310.

Housel, Morgan. "The Psychology of Money." Narrated by Chris Hil. Harriman House, Published September 8, 2020. Introduction 9:41. Audible audio ed. 5 hr., 48 min.

Housel, Morgan. "The Psychology of Money." Narrated by Chris Hil. Harriman House, Published September 8, 2020. Chapter 13 12:10. Audible audio ed. 5 hr., 48 min.

Investing.com. "GameStop Corp." Accessed October 6, 2021. https://www.investing.com/equities/gamestop-corp-historical-data.

Kenton, Will. "The S&P 500 Index: Standard & Poor's 500 Index." Investopedia. Accessed October 6, 2021. https://www.investopedia.com/terms/s/sp500.asp.

Lacurci, Gregg. "Money invested in ESG funds more than doubles in a year." CNBC. Updated February 11, 2021. https://www.cnbc.com/2021/02/11/sustainable-investment-funds-more-than-doubled-in-2020-.html.

The Next Web. "The 'average' Robinhood trader is no match for the S&P 500, just like Buffett." June 4, 2020. https://thenextweb.com/news/robinhood-trader-average-underperform-sp-500-index-like-warren-buffett.

Ponczek, Sarah. "Robinhood, Chronicler of Day Trader Stock Demand, to Shut." Bloomberg, Updated August 8, 2020. https://www.bloomberg.com/news/articles/2020-08-08/robintrack-chronicler-of-day-trader-stock-demand-to-shut-down.

Popper, Nathaniel. "Robinhood Has Lured Young Traders, Sometimes With Devastating Results." *The New York Times*, Updated September 5, 2021. https://www.nytimes.com/2020/07/08/technology/robinhood-risky-trading.html.

Principles for Responsible Investment. "What are the Principles for Responsible Investment?" Accessed October 6, 2021. https://www.unpri.org/pri/what-are-the-principles-for-responsible-investment.

Roberts, Jeff John. "Robinhood will no longer share stock 'popularity data' with sites like Robintrack." Fortune, August 10,

2020. https://fortune.com/2020/08/10/robinhood-populari-ty-data-robintrack-stock-market-trading-tracker/.

Chapter 8

Alden, Lyn. "3 Reasons I'm Investing in Bitcoin." Published July 16, 2020. https://www.lynalden.com/invest-in-bitcoin/.

Alden, Lyn. "7 Misconceptions About Bitcoin." Published November 11, 2020. https://www.lynalden.com/author/penumbra/

Britannica. "Gresham's Law." Accessed October 6, 2021. https://www.britannica.com/topic/Greshams-law.

Britannica. "Sir Thomas Gresham." Accessed October 6, 2021. https://www.britannica.com/biography/Thomas-Gresham.

Brown, Gavin and Richard Whittle. "More than 1,000 cryptocur-rencies have already failed—here's what will affect successes in future." Accessed October 6, 2021. https://theconversation.com/more-than-1-000-cryptocurrencies-have-already-failed-heres-what-will-affect-successes-in-future-127463.

CoinDesk. "Dogecoin." Accessed October 6, 2021. https://www.coindesk.com/price/dogecoin/.

Hayes, Adam. "Satoshi Nakamoto." Investopedia. Reviewed on July 21, 2021. https://www.investopedia.com/terms/s/satoshi-naka-moto.asp.

Kaur, Avneet. "2800% returns YTD! What's happening with Dogecoin?" BusinessToday. Updated May 8, 2021. https://

www.businesstoday.in/personal-finance/investment/sto-
ry/2800-percetn-returns-ytd-whats-happening-with-doge-
coin-293399-2021-04-14.

Luno. "Why are there only 21 million Bitcoin?" Accessed October
6, 2021. https://www.luno.com/learn/en/article/why-are-there-
only-million-bitcoin.

Mott, Nathaniel. "Woof: Dogecoin Cryptocurrency Returns Are
up 6,000% This Year." Tom's Hardware. April 16, 2021. https://
www.tomshardware.com/news/woof-dogecoin-cryptocurren-
cy-returns-are-up-6000-this-year.

Phillips, Daniel. "Why is Bitcoin's supply limit set to 21 million?"
Decrypt. December 30, 2020. https://decrypt.co/34876/why-is-
bitcoins-supply-limit-set-to-21-million.

Sofi. "Understanding The Different Types of Cryptocurrency." September 17, 2021. https://www.sofi.com/learn/content/under-
standing-the-different-types-of-cryptocurrency/.

Tardi, Carla. "Decentralized Market." Investopedia. Accessed
October 6, 2021. https://www.investopedia.com/terms/d/
decentralizedmarket.asp.

UpMyInterest. "Bitcoin—Bitcoin (Cryptocurrency)." Accessed
October 6, 2021. https://www.upmyinterest.com/fund?tick=Bit-
coin.

Wasik, John F. "Why So Many Cryptocurrencies Fail." Forbes, July
20, 2018. https://www.forbes.com/sites/johnwasik/2018/07/20/
why-so-many-cryptocurrencies-fail/?sh=823c4914b5e6.

Chapter 9

Bartash, Jeffry. "The US has only regained 42% of the 22 million jobs lost in the pandemic. Here's where they are." Market Watch, August 7th, 2020. https://www.marketwatch.com/story/restaurants-and-retailers-have-regained-the-most-jobs-since-the-coronavirus-crisis-but-theres-a-catch-2020-08-07.

Chen, James. "Federal Funds Rate." Investopedia. Accessed October 6, 2021. https://www.investopedia.com/terms/f/federalfundsrate.asp.

Powell, Jerome. Interview by Bill Owens. Bill Owens. April 11, 2021. https://www.cbs.com/shows/60_minutes/video/gEWdbn4XRIq_Fx1RkZqLccUuMXCoXIN8/fed-chairman-jerome-powell-the-2021-60-minutes-interview/.

Federal Reserve. "Federal Open Market Committee." Accessed October 6, 2021. https://www.federalreserve.gov/monetary-policy/fomc.htm.

Federal Reserve. "Interest on Reserve Balances." Accessed October 6, 2021. https://www.federalreserve.gov/monetarypolicy/reserve-balances.htm#:~:text=The%20interest%20rate%20on%20excess,the%20conduct%20of%20monetary%20policy.

Federal Reserve Bank of San Francisco. "Why did the Federal Reserve start paying interest on reserve balances held on deposit at the Fed? Does the Fed pay interest on required reserves, excess reserves, or both? What interest rate does the Fed pay?" March 2013. https://www.frbsf.org/education/

publications/doctor-econ/2013/march/federal-reserve-inter-est-balances-reserves/.

Federal Reserve Bank of St. Louis. "Making Sense of the Federal Reserve." Accessed October 6, 2021. https://www.stlouisfed.org/ in-plain-english/expansionary-and-contractionary-policy#:~:-text=The%20Fed%20can%20use%20four,operations%2C%20 and%20interest%20on%20reserves.

Hess, Abigail Johnson. "The US still has 10 million fewer jobs now than before the pandemic." CNBC. December 8, 2020. https:// www.cnbc.com/2020/12/08/the-us-has-10-million-fewer-jobs-now-than-before-the-pandemic.html.

Macrotrends. "Federal Funds Rate—Historical Annual Yield Data." Accessed October 6, 2021. https://www.macrotrends.net/2015/ fed-funds-rate-historical-chart.

Chapter 10

Baluch, Anna. "What Are the Different Types of Credit Scores?" Lendingtree. Updated October 22, 2020. https://www.lending-tree.com/credit-repair/what-are-the-different-types-of-credit-scores/.

Baluch, Anna. "What Is a Credit Score and How Is It Calculated?" Lendingtree. Updated September 30, 2020. https://www.lend-ingtree.com/credit-repair/what-are-the-different-types-of-credit-scores/.

Equifax. "Credit Scores." Accessed October 6, 2021. https://www. equifax.com/personal/education/credit/score/.

Federal Trade Commision. "Fair and Accurate Credit Transactions Act of 2003." https://www.ftc.gov/enforcement/statutes/fair-accurate-credit-transactions-act-2003.

Helhoski, Anna, Cecelia Clark, and Colin Beresford. "What is the FAFSA?" Nerdwallet. Accessed October 6, 2021. https://www.nerdwallet.com/l/nerdwallet-guide-to-fafsa.

Hollis, Casey. "What is a good credit score?" Credit Karma. Updated June 20, 2021. https://www.creditkarma.com/what-is-a-good-credit-score.

Investopedia. "The Top 3 Credit Bureaus." Updated April 28, 2021. https://www.investopedia.com/personal-finance/top-three-credit-bureaus/.

Kagan, Julia. "VantageScore." Investopedia. Updated September 13, 2020. https://www.investopedia.com/terms/v/vantagescore.asp.

Kurt, Daniel. "Student Loan Debt: 2021 Statistics and Outlook." Investopedia. Updated September 9, 2021. https://www.investopedia.com/student-loan-debt-2019-statistics-and-outlook-4772007.

Lee, Jeanne. "5 key steps in the mortgage underwriting process." Bankrate. March 15, 2021. https://www.bankrate.com/mortgages/steps-in-underwriting-process/.

Lowry, Erin. "Broke Millenial." Narrated by the author. Gildan Media, LLC, 2017. Chapter 6 10:42, 11:56, 42:41. Audible audio ed. 8 hr., 48 min.

Lowry, Erin. "Broke Millenial." Narrated by the author. Gildan
Media, LLC, 2017. Chapter 7 2:30. Audible audio ed. 8 hr., 48
min.

Lowry, Erin. "Broke Millenial." Narrated by the author. Gildan
Media, LLC, 2017. Chapter 9 6:41. Audible audio ed. 8 hr., 48
min.

Luthi, Ben. "What Is a Payday Loan and How Does It Work?"
Experian. January 3, 2019. https://www.experian.com/blogs/
ask-experian/how-payday-loans-work/.

Luthi, Ben and Kristen Hampshire. "What is Underwriting?" US
News & World Report, January 19, 2021. https://loans.usnews.
com/articles/what-is-loan-underwriting.

McCann, Adam. "Average Credit Card Interest Rates." WalletHub.
July 13, 2021. https://wallethub.com/edu/cc/average-cred-
it-card-interest-rate/50841.

Medine, Taylor. "What Is My VantageScore?" Lendingtree.
April 10, 2019. https://www.lendingtree.com/credit-repair/
what-is-my-vantagescore/.

MoneyWise. September 4, 2021. 10:10. Podcast.

My Fico. "What is a Credit Score?" Accessed October 6, 2021.
https://www.myfico.com/credit-education/credit-scores.

O'Shea, Bev. "9 Ways to Build Credit Fast." Nerdwallet. September
28, 2021. https://www.nerdwallet.com/article/finance/raise-
credit-score-fast.

Palmer, Barclay. "What Is PMI and Does Everyone Need to Pay It?" Investopedia. Reviewed June 30, 2021. https://www.investopedia.com/ask/answers/09/pmi.asp.

Sullivan, Tyler. "Jerry Jones has no regrets with Dak Prescott deal: Anything 'that ended up being special, I overpaid for'." CBS Sports March 10, 2021. https://www.cbssports.com/nfl/news/jerry-jones-has-no-regrets-with-dak-prescott-deal-anything-that-ended-up-being-special-i-overpaid-for/.

WalletHub." "How many points does a hard inquiry affect a credit score?" April 29, 2020. https://wallethub.com/answers/cs/how-many-points-does-a-hard-inquiry-affect-credit-score-2140706774/.

Chapter 11

Apstein, Stephanie. "An Oral History of Barry Bonds's Intentional Walk With the Bases Loaded." Sports Illustrated, May 28, 2020. https://www.si.com/mlb/2020/05/28/barry-bonds-intentional-walk-bases-loaded.

Baseball Reference. "Albert Pujuls." Accessed October 1, 2021. https://www.baseball-reference.com/players/p/pujolal01.shtml.

Baseball Reference. "Barry Bonds." Accessed October 1, 2021. https://www.baseball-reference.com/players/b/bondsba01.shtml.

Bloomer, Ester. "Here's how much the average American spends on health care." CNBC. Updated October 14, 2019. https://www.

cnbc.com/2017/06/23/heres-how-much-the-average-american-spends-on-health-care.html.

Bonner, Marianne. "Insurance Company Financial Ratings." The Balance. Updated January 15, 2002. https://www.thebalancesmb.com/insurance-company-ratings-462502.

Celebrity Net Worth. "Hank Aaron Net Worth." Accessed October 6, 2021. https://www.celebritynetworth.com/richest-athletes/richest-baseball/hank-aaron-net-worth/.

Cms.gov. "National Health Expenditures 2017 Highlights." Accessed October 6, 2021. https://www.cms.gov/research-statistics-data-and-systems/statistics-trends-and-reports/nationalhealthexpenddata/downloads/highlights.pdf.

Costhelper. "How Much Does an Emergency Room Visit Cost?" Accessed October 6, 2021. https://health.costhelper.com/emergency-room.html.

Gough, Christina. "Major League Baseball—highest paid players 2021." statista, Published March 2, 2021. https://www.statista.com/statistics/533971/highest-paid-mlb-players/.

Holzworth, Larry. "Some Baffling Insurance Policies Issued by Lloyd's of London." History Collect. November 13, 2019. https://historycollection.com/some-baffling-insurance-policies-issued-by-lloyds-of-london/14/.

Kagan, Julia. "Insurance Company Credit Rating." Investopedia. Accessed October 6, 2021. https://www.investopedia.com/terms/i/insurance-company-credit-rating.asp.

Kamal, Rabah, Daniel McDermott, Gianorlando, Cynthia Cox. "How has U.S. spending on healthcare changed over time?" Health System Tracker. Published December 23, 2020. https://www.healthsystemtracker.org/chart-collection/u-s-spending-healthcare-changed-time/#item-start.

Marcus, Steven. "Hank Aaron recalls racism during his chase for Babe Ruth's home run record." Newsday, February 2, 2019. https://www.newsday.com/sports/baseball/hank-aaron-black-history-month-1.26740392.

MLB. "D-backs walk Bonds with the bases loaded." May 27, 2015. Video, 3:09. https://www.youtube.com/watch?v=xi7IPZAcP78.

Porretta, Anna. "How Much Does Individual Health Insurance Cost? Ehealth. Updated November 24, 2020. https://www.ehealthinsurance.com/resources/individual-and-family/how-much-does-individual-health-insurance-cost.

US Department of Health and Human Services. Access October 6, 2021. https://www.hhs.gov/healthcare/about-the-aca/benefit-limits/index.html.

Wilson, Louis. "The 10 craziest things insured at Lloyd's of London." Haven Life. May 21, 2018. https://havenlife.com/blog/craziest-things-insured-lloyds-london/.

Wolstenholm, Jack. "How to check insurance company ratings for financial strength." Breeze. Updated January 4, 2021. https://www.meetbreeze.com/blog/insurance-company-ratings/.

Young, Jabari. "Why Trevor Bauer's $102 million deal with the Dodgers is unique." CNBC. February 12, 2021. https://www.cnbc.com/2021/02/12/trevor-bauers-102-million-deal-with-the-dodgers-is-unique-heres-why.html.

Chapter 12

Crosby, Daniel. "The Behavioral Investor." Narrated by Matthew R. Doyle. Harriman House Ltd., 2019. Chapter 12 36:56. Audible audio ed. 8 hr., 23 min.

Internal Revenue Service. "Credits and Deductions for Individuals." Accessed October 6, 2021. https://www.irs.gov/credits-deductions-for-individuals.

Medical News Today. "What is decision fatigue?" Reviewed March 16, 2020. https://www.medicalnewstoday.com/articles/decision-fatigue.

Pfau, Dr. Wade. "Determining Sustainable Spending from an Investment Portfolio in Retirement." Retirement Researcher. Accessed October 6, 2021. https://retirementresearcher.com/determining-sustainable-spending-from-an-investment-portfolio-in-retirement/.

Ross, Sean. "Elon Musk's Best Investments." Investopedia. Updated May 15, 2021. https://www.investopedia.com/articles/investing/031316/elon-musks-5-best-investments-tsla-pypl.asp.

Silva, Derek. "53 tax deductions & tax credits you can take in 2021." Policygenius. Updated February 5, 2021. https://www.policygenius.com/taxes/tax-deductions-tax-credits-you-can-take/.

Taylor, Todd, Nick Halen, and Dyan Huang. "The Decumulation Paradox." Investments and Wealth Monitor. Reprinted from July/August 2018. https://investmentsandwealth.org/getattachment/2eb24816-5980-4e10-865b-df4e80acb2e9/IWM18JulAug-DecumulationParadox.pdf?_sm_au_=iVVQ4V5WZ466NTcjjfco6K6ttCjRt.

Chapter 13

"Anna Nicole Smith: The Mother Of All Estate Litigation Cases." Talbot Law Group, P.C. Published July 16, 2015. https://www.matthewbtalbot.com/blog/2015/7/16/anna-nicole-smith-the-mother-of-all-estate-litigation-cases.

Blue, Ron. "Splitting Heirs." Chicago, IL: Northfield Publishing, 2008.

Cobb, Daniel. "For the First Time, Caring.com's Wills Survey Finds that Younger Adults Are More Likely to Have a Will than Middle-Aged Adults." Caring.com. Accessed October 6, 2021. https://www.caring.com/caregivers/estate-planning/wills-survey/.

de Vougue, Ariane. "Supreme Court Rules in Anna Nicole Smith's 15-Year Legal Battle." ABC News, June 23, 2011. https://abcnews.go.com/Politics/supreme-court-rules-anna-nicole-smiths-15-year/story?id=13913522.

Itzkoff, Dave. "Inside the Final Days of Robin Williams." Vanity Fair, May 8, 2018. https://www.vanityfair.com/hollywood/2018/05/robin-williams-death-biography-dave-itzkoff-excerpt.

Lumpkins Walls, Barbranda. "Haven't Done A Will Yet?" AARP.
February 24, 2017. https://www.aarp.org/money/investing/
info-2017/half-of-adults-do-not-have-wills.html.

"The Story Of How Anna Nicole Smith Thought She Deserved To
Inherit 8% Of Koch Industries." Wealth Advisor. September
1, 2020. https://www.thewealthadvisor.com/article/story-how-
anna-nicole-smith-thought-she-deserved-inherit-8-koch-in-
dustries.

Stout, David. "Anna Nicole Smith Wins Supreme Court
Case." New York Times, May 1, 2006. https://www.nytimes.
com/2006/05/01/washington/01cnd-smith.html.

Youn Soo. "Robin Williams: Autopsy Confirms Death by Suicide."
The Hollywood Reporter, November 7, 2014. https://www.hol-
lywoodreporter.com/news/general-news/robin-williams-au-
topsy-confirms-death-746194/.

Chapter 14

Albrecht, Leslie. "Charitable giving rose in 2020, depsite financial turmoil from COVID-19—Why did Americans show such
gnerosity?" Market Watch. Updated February 22, 2021. https://
www.marketwatch.com/story/charitable-giving-rose-in-2020-
despite-financial-turmoil-from-covid-19-why-did-americans-
show-such-generosity-11613662427.

Blackbaud Institute. "Overall Giving Trends." Accessed October 6,
2021. https://institute.blackbaud.com/charitable-giving-report/
overall-giving-trends/.

National Philanthropic Trust. "NPT curates statistics from recent studies and reports on charitable giving in the US Please refer to the footnotes for original sources." Accessed October 6, 2021. https://www.nptrust.org/philanthropic-resources/charitable-giving-statistics/#:~:text=General%20Philanthropy,a%20 5.1%25%20increase%20from%202018.&text=Corporate%20giving%20in%202019%20increased,a%2013.4%25%20increase%20 from%202018.&text=Foundation%20giving%20in%202019%20 increased,a%202.5%25%20increase%20from%202018.

Chapter 15

Clifford, Colby. "Apple's worst failures of all time, from AirPower to Bendgate to the Newton." Cnet, April 2, 2019. https://www.cnet.com/tech/mobile/apples-worst-failures-of-all-time-from-airpower-to-bendgate-to-the-newton/.

Corporate Finance Insittute. "What are SMART Goals?" Accessed October 6, 2021. https://corporatefinanceinstitute.com/resources/knowledge/other/smart-goal/.

Entrepreneur. "Steve Jobs: An Extraordinary Career." Updated April 1, 2021. https://www.entrepreneur.com/article/197538.

Ferkun Gal, Selim. "5 Most Failed Apple Products in History." Medium. February 17, 2021. https://medium.com/technology-hits/5-most-failed-apple-products-in-history-c6ba84aaf36b

Gallo, Carmine. "5 Reasons Why Steve Jobs's iPhone Keynote Is Still the Best Presentation of All Time." Inc., June 29, 2017. https://www.inc.com/carmine-gallo/5-reasons-why-steve-jobs-iphone-keynote-is-still-the-best-presentation-of-all-ti.html.

Haughey, Jason. "SMART Goals." ProjectSmart. Accessed October 6, 2021. https://www.projectsmart.co.uk/smart-goals.php.

Kroll, Jacob. "The new iPad Pro and iMac are up for preorder — here's your guide." CNN, Updated April 3, 2021. https://www.cnn.com/2021/04/20/cnn-underscored/imac-ipad-pro-airtags-preorders.

Mind Tools. "SMART Goals How to Make Your Goals Achievable." Accessed October 6, 2021. https://www.mindtools.com/pages/article/smart-goals.htm.

Mitchell, Houston. "Steve Jobs used Wayne Gretzky as inspiration." Los Angeles Times, October 6, 2011. https://latimesblogs.latimes.com/sports_blog/2011/10/steve-jobs-used-wayne-gretzky-as-inspiration.html.

Moon, Brad. "Apple's 12 Biggest Product Flops of All Time." Kiplinger, February 14, 2019. https://www.kiplinger.com/slideshow/investing/t058-s001-apple-s-12-biggest-flops-of-all-time/index.html.

Moss, Caroline. "From The 'Apple Lisa' To The U2 iPod: Apple Products That Totally Flopped." Business Insider, November 5, 2013. https://www.businessinsider.com/10-old-apple-products-that-totally-failed-2013-11.

Rambo, Guilherme. "Apple officially unveils AirTag item tracker." 9To5Mac, April 20, 2021. https://9to5mac.com/2021/04/20/apple-officially-unveils-airtag-item-tracker/.

Robin, Vicki and Joe Dominguez. "Your Money or Your Life." New York, NY: Penguin Books, 2008.

Simon, Michael. "Apple at 40: Remembering when Steve Jobs went electric." Macworld, April 3, 2016. https://www.macworld.com/article/227736/apple-at-40-remembering-when-steve-jobs-went-electric.html.

Tang, Terry. "How to have a clear vision like Steve Jobs for Apple." Averagers. Updated Jul4 14, 2019. https://averagers.com/how-to-have-a-clear-vision-like-steve-jobs-for-apple/.

Your Money Your Life. "WELCOME TO YOUR MONEY OR YOUR LIFE | LIFE > MONEY." Accessed October 6, 2021. https://yourmoneyoryourlife.com/about/.

Chapter 16

Classic Reload. "Number Munchers." Accessed October 26, 2021. https://classicreload.com/number-munchers.html.

Fernando, Jason. "Financial Literacy." Investopedia. Accessed October 26, 2021. https://www.investopedia.com/terms/f/financial-literacy.asp.

Flatley, Kerry. 17 Fun Money Activities for Kids." Self-sufficient Kids. Accessed October 26, 2021. https://selfsufficientkids.com/17-fun-money-activities-for-kids/.

Huddleston, Cameron. "How To Teach Your Kids Good Money Habits." Forbes, Updated February 18, 2020. https://www.

forbes.com/advisor/personal-finance/how-to-teach-your-kids-good-money-habits/.

Intuit Mint Life. "40 Financial Statistics for 2021." Modified June 11, 2021. https://mint.intuit.com/blog/financial-literacy/financial-statistics/.

Kesmodel, David. "Meet the Father of Zero-Based Budgeting." The Wall Street Journal, March 26, 2015. https://www.wsj.com/articles/meet-the-father-of-zero-based-budgeting-1427415074.

Kilmashousky, Danielle. "The Top 10 Financial Certifications." Smart Asset, May 1, 2020. https://smartasset.com/financial-advisor/top-10-financial-certifications.

Sagevest Kids. "15 Fun Money Activities for Kids." June 18, 2019. https://www.kidsfinancialeducation.com/15-fun-money-activities-for-kids/.

Turkle, Shelly. "Alone Together." Narrated by Laural Merlington. Basic Books, Published October 2, 2012. Conclusion 18:52, 44:19. Audible audio ed. 14 hr., 45 min.

Chapter 17

AP News. "75-year Harvard study: what makes us happy?" April 21, 2019. https://apnews.com/article/6dab1e79c-34e4514af8d184d951f5733.

Berger, Michele. "Money matters to happiness—perhaps more than previously thought." Penn Today, anuary 18, 2021. https://

penntoday.upenn.edu/news/money-matters-to-happiness-per-haps-more-than-previously-thought.

Curtin, Melanie. "This 75-Year Harvard Study Found the 1 Secret to Leading a Fulfilling Life." Inc., August 31, 2021. https://www.inc.com/melanie-curtin/want-a-life-of-fulfillment-a-75-year-harvard-study-says-to-prioritize-this-one-t.html.

Fulghum Bruce, Dr. Debra. "Exercise and Depression." WebMD. Accessed October 26, 2021. https://www.webmd.com/depression/guide/exercise-depression.

Greene, Robert. "The Laws of Human Nature." Read by Paul Michael and the author. Penguin Books, Published October 1, 2019. Chapter 5 2:00. Audible audio ed. 28 hr., 26 min.

Greene, Robert. "The Laws of Human Nature." Read by Paul Michael and the author. Penguin Books, Published October 1, 2019. Chapter 7 1:55. Audible audio ed. 28 hr., 26 min.

Hill, Catey. "This common behavior is the No. 1 predictor of whether you'll get divorced." Market Watch, January 10, 2018. https://www.marketwatch.com/story/this-common-behavior-is-the-no-1-predictor-of-whether-youll-get-divorced-2018-01-10.

Holland, Kelley. "Fighting with your spouse? It's probably about this." CNBC, Updated February 4, 2015. https://www.cnbc.com/2015/02/04/money-is-the-leading-cause-of-stress-in-relationships.html.

Luscombe, Belinda. "Do We Need $75,000 a Year to Be Happy?" Time, December 6, 2010. http://content.time.com/time/magazine/article/0,9171,2019628,00.html#.

Martin, Emmie. "Here's how much money you need to be happy, according to a new analysis by wealth experts." CNBC, Updated November 20, 2017. https://www.cnbc.com/2017/11/20/how-much-money-you-need-to-be-happy-according-to-wealth-experts.html.

Mineo, Liz. "Good genes are nice, but joy is better." The Harvard Gazette, April 11, 2017. https://news.harvard.edu/gazette/story/2017/04/over-nearly-80-years-harvard-study-has-been-showing-how-to-live-a-healthy-and-happy-life/.

Ngendo, Virginia. "Famous Socrates quotes on life, love, and change." Legit, November 17, 2019. https://www.legit.ng/1275919-famous-socrates-quotes-life-love-change.html.

Solan, Matthew. "The secret to happiness? Here's some advice from the longest-running study on happiness." Harvard Health Publishing. October 5, 2017. https://www.health.harvard.edu/blog/the-secret-to-happiness-heres-some-advice-from-the-longest-running-study-on-happiness-2017100512543.

Stieg, Corey. "How you think about money can impact how happy you are in life, study says." CNBC, September 5, 2019. https://www.cnbc.com/2019/09/05/can-money-buy-happiness-debate-study-on-success.html.

Stieg, Corey. "People actually are happier when they make more money: Wharton study." CNBC, Updated January 22, 2021.

https://www.cnbc.com/2021/01/22/new-wharton-study-people-are-happier-when-they-earn-more-money.html.

Turkle, Shelly. "Alone Together." Narrated by Laural Merlington. Basic Books, Published October 2, 2012. Conclusion 42:52, 43:25. Audible audio ed. 14 hr., 45 min.

US News and World Report. "Odds Are $1.5 Billion Powerball Winner Will End Up Bankrupt." January 12, 2016. https://www.usnews.com/news/articles/2016/01/12/odds-are-15-billion-powerball-winner-will-end-up-bankrupt.

Wolf Shank, Joshua. "What Makes Us Happy?" The Atlantic, June 2009. https://www.theatlantic.com/magazine/archive/2009/06/what-makes-us-happy/307439/.